PRACTICAL HANDBOOK

COMPLETE GUIDE TO
BIRD CARE

2008

PRACTICAL HANDBOOK

COMPLETE GUIDE TO
BIRD CARE

DAVID ALDERTON

LORENZ BOOKS

This edition is published by Lorenz Books

Lorenz Books is an imprint of Anness Publishing Ltd
Hermes House, 88–89 Blackfriars Road, London SE1 8HA
tel. 020 7401 2077; fax 020 7633 9499; www.lorenzbooks.com; info@anness.com

© Anness Publishing Ltd 2001, 2003

UK agent: The Manning Partnership Ltd, 6 The Old Dairy, Melcombe Road, Bath BA2 3LR
tel. 01225 478 444; fax 01225 478 440; sales@manning-partnership.co.uk

UK distributor: Grantham Book Services Ltd, Isaac Newton Way, Alma Park Industrial Estate, Grantham, Lincs NG31 9SD
tel. 01476 541080; fax 01476 541061; orders@gbs.tbs-ltd.co.uk

North American agent/distributor: National Book Network, 4501 Forbes Boulevard, Suite 200, Lanham, MD 20706
tel. 301 459 3366; fax 301 429 5746; www.nbnbooks.com

Australian agent/distributor: Pan Macmillan Australia, Level 18, St Martins Tower, 31 Market St, Sydney, NSW 2000
tel. 1300 135 113; fax 1300 135 103; customer.service@macmillan.com.au

A CIP catalogue record for this book is available from the British Library.

Publisher Joanna Lorenz
Managing Editor Judith Simons
Project Editor Sarah Ainley
Designer Michael Morey
Photographer John Daniels
Index Helen Snaith

Previously published as part of a larger volume, *The Ultimate Encyclopedia of Caged and Aviary Birds*.

1 3 5 7 9 10 8 6 4 2

Bracketed terms are intended for American readers.

Contents

BIRD CARE AND MANAGEMENT   6

Starting Out   10

Accommodation   16

Foods and their Uses   36

Caring for a Pet Bird   52

Caring for Aviary Birds   60

Buying Birds   68

Keeping Birds Healthy   78

The Show Scene   90

Breeding Birds   98

GLOSSARY   124

ACKNOWLEDGEMENTS   126

FURTHER READING   127

INDEX   128

BIRD CARE AND MANAGEMENT

INTRODUCTION

◆ BELOW
The budgerigar is the most popular pet bird in the world today, thanks to its friendly nature, and the ease with which it can be kept in a home environment.

Birds have been popular as pets for at least 4,000 years, dating back to the time of the ancient Egyptians. Today, their appeal as companions spans the globe. The talking abilities of parrots, for instance, enchants owners living in stylish apartments in Paris, New York or London as much as tribespeople living in scattered village communities across the Amazon basin or in the rain forests of West Africa. When European settlers arrived in Australia in the 1700s they started to keep one of the smaller native parakeets as pets. Since then, these birds, better known as budgerigars, have become the most widely kept pet birds in the world.

It is not just their powers of mimicry, however, that have attracted people to keeping birds as companions; the song of the canary was responsible for the introduction of these rather plain-coloured, greenish finches to Europe in the late 1400s, from the Canary Islands off the west coast of Africa. Now, domestic canaries possess singing abilities that are vastly superior to those of

their wild relatives. Canaries have also evolved into birds displaying a wide range of colours; many distinctive varieties have been developed, which are popular for exhibition purposes. The exotic appearance and coloration of softbills and finches underlies their popularity. They are a constant source of fascination in a suitable aviary, and the challenge of breeding such birds successfully appeals to many people. The same applies to pheasants and doves and these will thrive in a planted aviary.

Caring for birds has become more straightforward over recent years, thanks to a better understanding of their nutritional needs.

◆ ABOVE
A young budgerigar chick being hand-reared. Such birds will be very tame once they are weaned. They usually display no fear of people, and make ideal pets in the home.

✦ BELOW
Budgerigars are now bred in a huge range of
colour varieties and are popular exhibition
birds. Here a group are being bred on a colony
basis in an aviary.

Special foods for all types of birds, ranging from humming-birds to flamingos, are produced commercially, with each one formulated to match particular needs. This, in turn, has been valuable in persuading pairs to breed successfully. Better general health means that if a bird does fall ill there is a greater chance of recovery. Advances in the field of equipment have helped to revolutionize the housing of birds, which contributes to their overall well-being.

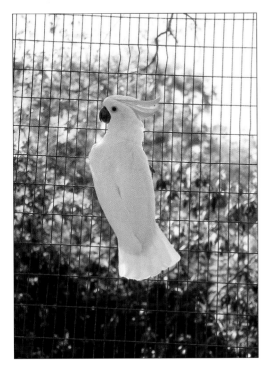

Many people start out with a single pet bird and before long decide to construct an aviary. The exhibition side of the hobby often appeals to people once they have experience of bird breeding. Local clubs, catering for all types of birds, usually stage an annual show, and these provide an ideal way to meet fellow-enthusiasts in your area, even if you are not interested in exhibiting. National groups cater for particular types of birds, such as parrots or budgerigars, and the larger ones may operate through local branches. They usually produce an annual newsletter or magazine for their members, keeping them up-to-date with the latest information and details of shows. You can track down information about local or national clubs through the columns of the bird-keeping publications, your local library or via the Internet.

✦ LEFT
Parrots such as cockatoos are not only costly to purchase, but are difficult to accommodate in view of their destructive natures. They can also prove to be very noisy, as is the case with many large birds.

9

STARTING OUT

Once you have decided to keep a bird as a pet, it is vital to consider the options before committing yourself to a particular species, or you could choose one that is unsuitable for a variety of reasons – it may not settle in your home environment, or it may be noisy, leading to complaints from the neighbours. Having to find a new home for the bird soon after acquiring it is likely to be traumatic for all concerned, especially for a bird that is used to human company.

It can help to draw up a checklist. Consider such things as the bird's talking ability, how easy or demanding it is to look after, its lifespan, as well as its accommodation requirements, and whether it is particularly destructive.

Your budget is another important consideration. Suitable housing for any bird is likely to be more expensive than the bird itself. If you cannot afford both at the same time, never be tempted to buy the bird immediately and keep it confined in less than ideal surroundings. It may start to pluck its feathers as a consequence, and this can easily become an habitual problem. Wait until you can afford both together.

The price of birds does vary. A young, hand-reared parrot chick may cost almost twice as much as an older, untamed bird, but if you are seeking a pet, it really will pay dividends to select a young one that has been reared in the home. There is also a wide price variance among exhibition birds, because of their pedigrees, and it pays to research carefully, to be sure of obtaining the best value for money.

◆ OPPOSITE
It is worthwhile constructing an aviary
in a part of your garden where it can be
expanded if your interest in bird-keeping
develops over time.

◆ LEFT
Finches prove to be attractive and lively
aviary occupants, thriving in a planted
setting. Many, such as the Bengalese or
society finch seen here, will breed well
in these surroundings.

PLANNING AHEAD

Although birds are less demanding to look after than some pets, such as dogs, they still need to be cared for every day throughout the year. This is something to be considered right at the outset, before you finalize your choice of bird species.

It is usually not too difficult to find a friend or neighbour prepared to look after the bird while you are away, although it is not necessarily a good idea to leave the bird, especially a parrot, at home on its own for most of the time, particularly if you are going to be absent for longer than a day or two. It is likely to start to pine for company, having been used to constant contact with people. Parrots are highly social by nature, which is why they settle so well as companion birds, forming a strong bond with their owners. A change in their

routine, especially when it results in isolation and boredom, can be sufficient to trigger feather plucking. Once this problem develops, it can be very difficult to cure, even if the underlying stress is subsequently removed. Rather than arranging for someone to call in your absence, it is better if the bird is moved to their home, where it will have regular company. Try to avoid a friend who has a cat – there is always a chance that the bird will slip out of its quarters, while it is being fed or cleaned out, with disastrous consequences.

If you have a collection of birds, consider asking someone to stay while you are away, in order to look after them all. This is the least disruptive option. Professional house-sitters are available in some areas, if it's not convenient for friends

or relatives, but employing one of these will, of course, add to the cost of your trip.

In the case of aviary birds, you may be able to persuade a neighbour to feed and water seed-eating birds without too much trouble, but caring for softbills, with their more specific dietary needs, can present problems. One solution is to team up with another bird-keeper in the area, and arrange to look after each other's collections when either of you is away. A problem may arise if you both have to be away at the same time, but there may be someone else from the local bird club who will be prepared to help out. Forward planning is important; bear in mind when you book your holiday that at certain times of the year, such as Christmas, people are less likely to be able to help out.

✦ LEFT
A typical parrot cage, suitable for housing smaller members of this popular bird group in the home.

✦ ABOVE
Small finches are amongst the easiest birds to accommodate in an aviary, since they are neither noisy nor destructive by nature.

DOMESTIC CONSIDERATIONS

The bird's size is an important consideration, especially if you plan to keep it indoors, because of the size of the accommodation it will require. It is, for example, much easier to accommodate a Hahn's macaw (*Ara nobilis*), which measures barely 33 cm (13 in) long, than one of its larger relatives, such as the green-winged macaw (*A. chloroptera*), which is about 90 cm (36 in) in length. Even if the bird is going to spend most of its time out of its quarters, you still need to have a cage where it can be kept safely when you are away from home. Playstands take up space, and the bigger the bird, the bigger the playstand. Smaller species tend to be less noisy than their larger relatives, as well as being easier to restrain if you do not have any experience of handling birds.

Before you can let a newly homed bird out of its quarters, you will need to make a thorough check of the room from the point of view of the bird's safety. Choose one room in the house in which to release the bird, and prepare it carefully. The length of time that a bird spends out of its cage will depend on you; it is not recommended to leave the bird at liberty on its own. Although you will have dealt with the obvious dangers, there may be others, such as flaking lead paintwork, that are less obvious.

✦ RIGHT
Yellow-faced parrotlets are an ideal choice for a garden aviary, with pairs being quite likely to nest readily in such surroundings. They are also relatively hardy once established in their quarters outdoors.

Look at your garden from a suitable
vantage point and try to visualize
how the aviary will look when it is
in position. There needs to be easy
access, preferably via a path. Avoid
choosing an area which offers no room
for expansion. Bird-keeping often
proves to be an infectious hobby, and
there can be considerable savings in
cost if you can adapt an existing aviary
set-up when expanding your
collection, rather than having to build
another from scratch.

In temperate areas, winter-time
care is an important consideration –
not all birds are sufficiently hardy
to winter outdoors. An indoor
birdroom which forms part of the
aviary provides snug, winter-time
accommodation. Alternatively,
assemble an indoor aviary in a spare
room and move the birds into the
house. If you have a couple of pairs
of finches, however, housing them
in a spacious flight cage will be a
simpler option.

AVIARY CONSIDERATIONS

If you are planning an aviary you will
need to work out how large an area
you are prepared to devote to it, and
where it should be positioned in the
garden. It should be quite close to the
house, particularly if you are intending
to keep finches or softbills, so that if
you want to extend your domestic
electricity supply to provide additional
lighting and heating, it can be done
fairly easily and cheaply. However, it is
important to site the aviary so that it
will not upset the neighbours, who
may not appreciate the sound of bird
song outside their bedroom windows
at the crack of dawn.

It helps to choose a level site that is
not overhung by trees. These may
provide shade during the summer, but
leaves are likely to accumulate on the
roof in the autumn, possibly blocking
the guttering, and any branches that
break off are likely to damage the
structure, as well as scaring the
occupants of the aviary.

The greatest danger posed by
overhanging trees, however, comes

from wild birds roosting in their
branches. Droppings are likely to fall
down through the mesh and these can
introduce infections into the aviary.
Squirrels, too, can be a hazard,
clambering over the aviary from the
trees above. They may damage the
structure with their teeth, allowing
the birds to escape as a consequence.

A birdroom is very
useful, especially
if you are interested
in breeding
exhibition stock,
as these birds need
to be housed in
individual pairs for
breeding. It may be
possible to convert
an existing garden
building, such as
a shed, into
a birdroom.

You may be able to adapt an
existing garden building, a disused
garden shed for example, to make an
aviary or birdroom. This can reduce
the costs of setting up, but make sure
that the existing structure is sound.

Once the birds have settled in and
started nesting, it is difficult to carry
out major repairs. Brick or blockwork
structures are preferable because they
are durable. They are ideal for parrot
housing, in particular.

CLIMATIC CONSIDERATIONS

In various parts of the world, specific factors have to be borne in mind when
planning an aviary.

● In hot climates, it may be preferable to have an open-fronted shelter (which
can also reduce building costs). Birds can be housed outdoors but there must be
adequate protection for them during tropical downpours, with the floor of the
aviary being designed so that water will drain away quickly. If a bird becomes
waterlogged and falls to the floor, it could drown.

● Wooden structures are vulnerable to attacks by termites, so additional
investment in brick or blockwork designs is advisable in areas where they
proliferate.

● Aviaries must be secured against possible hurricane damage in areas
where they occur.

● Snakes will readily enter aviaries, taking chicks or even adult
birds, which will be particularly vulnerable in nest boxes.
Make sure the size of the mesh takes this into account.

● In colder climates, invest not just in heating but in
removable transparent plastic screening which fits around
the sides of the aviary to protect the occupants from the worst of
the wind chill. It is not a good idea to expose birds to very cold
conditions, because aside from the obvious risk of frostbite,
there can be insidious damage, particularly to the kidneys,
which ultimately could serve to shorten their lives.

◆ ABOVE
Even smaller members of the parrot family,
such as this Hahn's macaw, are likely to be
destructive. They are relatively hardy once
acclimatized, especially if provided with a
nest box for roosting purposes.

ACCOMMODATION

The choice of bird housing is large, and it is worthwhile finding a local store specializing in birds, or even a bird farm, where a good selection of flights and cages will be on view. Space is especially important and indoor cages should be as large as possible. A flight cage is a better option than a traditional cage, even if the bird is going to spend lengthy periods out of its quarters with you.

Aviaries are sold ready for home assembly. Most are of rectangular design, comprising a mesh-covered flight and a smaller shelter area, where the birds are fed and to which they can retreat in bad weather. They come in sectional form, so you can construct a structure of virtually any size. You can, of course, build your own aviary, although this will be more expensive. If you want something a little more unusual, there are elaborate options available, ranging from hi-tech octagonal designs to precise copies of ornate Victorian architecture.

If you intend to establish an exhibition stud, or have decided to keep the more delicate finches and softbills, a birdroom is a good idea. It will offer more space for breeding cages and for indoor flights, where birds can be housed in winter.

◆ OPPOSITE
Think carefully about where to site your aviary. Choose a sheltered, well-screened locality, which will help to protect the birds from cold winds.

◆ LEFT
A birdroom will provide an indoor area for housing less hardy birds during the winter. Attaching the birdroom to the aviary will make the set-up very convenient to use.

INDOOR QUARTERS

A wide selection of cage designs is now available for pet birds in the home. This means you are more likely to find a cage to blend in with your interior decor, but it also means you could be sold a cage that is more ornate than functional, and does not follow recommended guidelines.

Worse still, spending a lot of money is no guarantee that the cage will be suitable. It always helps to visit one of the larger pet superstores or a specialist bird farm, where a good selection of cages will be on view, and you will be able to ask advice from trained staff.

CHOOSING A FLIGHT CAGE

Always select a large flight cage. By providing your pet bird with plenty of space for exercise, you will help it to remain fit; obesity is a health risk and it can shorten a bird's life. In the home birds use relatively little energy to maintain their body temperature, and this, combined with lack of opportunity to exercise, means that they will put on weight rapidly. This, in turn, means that they will have progressive difficulty in flying, partly due to their excess weight, but also because their flight muscles will have become weakened through lack of use.

◆ ABOVE
This type of cage is used for either a pet budgerigar or canary. Budgerigars and other parrots prefer cages with horizontal bars, which makes it easier for them to climb around their quarters.

◆ LEFT
A small parrot cage, suitable for a Senegal parrot, for example. The bird should be let out of the cage each day for a period of exercise.

◆ RIGHT
The size of flight cages means they can be difficult to move around. Castors on the legs will be a great help.

◆ LEFT
Cages with vertical bars are most suitable
for finches and canaries, which do not climb
around their quarters. The perches need to be
placed near the raised food pots in this case.

It is no coincidence that birds housed in spacious surroundings are far less vulnerable to feather plucking than those housed in cages. If kept closely confined, parrots in particular will often suffer badly from boredom, and are likely to react in this way.

There are a number of spacious and stylish cage designs available. Those mounted on castors are preferable,

because they are easier to move. This helps with cleaning and if you want to transfer the parrot from one room to another. Wheeling the cage is more convenient and less disturbing for the bird than carrying it, especially if the cage is large and heavy.

The metal surfaces of bird cages are usually coated with a tough, easy-wipe covering. This makes them easy to clean, especially as there are special wipes available from good suppliers, intended for use on bird cages. This covering prolongs the life of the cage, preventing it from rusting.

In the case of mynah birds, because of their messy feeding habits, you should opt for a box-type flight cage,

rather than one with open-mesh sides. This will help to keep the environment around the cage cleaner.

It is a good idea to start looking for suitable accommodation well in advance of acquiring your pet, simply because you may not immediately be able to obtain the unit you want. It might be that the pet store has a suitable model, but that the colour is not ideal for your home, which will necessitate a different cage being ordered specially for you. When looking for bird housing, visit larger pet stores and bird farms in your area, where you are likely to see a better selection on display; remember, too, that a large price tag is no guarantee of a comfortable home for your pet.

◆ RIGHT
Not all cages are
designed with
much thought for
the needs of the
occupants. This
model provides
very little space,
and cannot be
recommended
for any bird.

◆ LEFT
Remember to
close the cage door
securely when a bird
is returned to its
cage after a period
of exercise, to
prevent escape. In
the case of parrots,
you may also need to
reinforce the door
catch with a padlock.

◆ LEFT
Provide wooden rather than plastic perches for
all birds. Parrots, such as this grey, gnaw their
perches, which will need to be replaced over
time, but the activity will keep its bill in trim.

PERCHES

The almost universal inclusion of plastic perches in flight cages is a serious flaw. Although in theory these perches are easy to keep clean, it is possible for their hollow interiors to become home to the red mite parasite. They are especially unsuitable for members of the parrot family. Parrots naturally keep their bills in trim by gnawing at branches, and the plastic perches will not stand up to it.

Some birds appear to find their ridged design uncomfortable after a period of time, probably because, being of an even diameter, they offer no variety in perching grip. The birds then resort to spending more time clinging on to the sides of their quarters. You must therefore be prepared to replace plastic perches at the outset.

Dowel perches are sometimes supplied with cages but these, too, have the drawback of being of a constant diameter. They do not appear to cause the birds as much discomfort as plastic perches, however, and they can be scrubbed off easily. Larger parrots are quite capable of gnawing them through, though, which means they will have to be replaced often.

Natural branches, cut from non-poisonous trees such as apple, are the best choice as perches, but do not use wood that may have been sprayed recently. Parrots especially will gnaw the bark and may swallow some of the slivers, in which case they could poison themselves. Sycamore is a good choice because it is relatively hard and grows straight, so that it is quite easy to cut perches to the requisite length. Elder is softer than sycamore and provides an outlet for parrots at their most destructive, although its gnarled bark makes it harder to clean than sycamore. In all cases, it is a good idea to wash off branches before placing them in the bird's quarters, just in case they may have been spoiled by wild birds previously.

When cutting branches to fit in a flight cage, allow for an overlap at the ends in order to hold the branches firmly in place. If you use wire to fix the perch, make sure that this is located safely outside the cage. Do not use string because this could choke a bird if it swallows any of the fibres, and there is also a risk of the bird becoming entangled.

The width of the perch is important. The diameter should be sufficiently broad to allow the bird to sit comfortably, without its front claws coming into direct contact with its rear toes. If not, the bird may encounter difficulties in perching easily, and if its sharp claws puncture the undersurface of the rear toes, there is a risk, especially in mynah birds, that an infection could develop. If budgerigars are kept in cages with perches of constant diameter, pressure sores will develop, and these are likely to become infected, creating the condition often described as bumblefoot. Even if the perching facilities are improved at this stage, treatment of the condition is likely to be difficult, because of its deep-seated nature, with the situation being made worse if the bird is obese because of lack of exercise.

WOOD FOR PERCHES

Use these:
Apple
Sycamore
Elder

Avoid these:
Laburnum
Lilac
Yew

DOOR FASTENINGS

A point of weakness in parrot cages is the door fastening. A simple hook will present little by way of a challenge to these intelligent birds, allowing them to escape into the room in your absence, with potentially serious consequences. Aside from the risk to furniture, a parrot may turn its attention to live electrical flex and electrocute itself as a result. It is always a good idea to reinforce the door fastening by means of a combination padlock, which the parrot will have much greater difficulty in opening.

In most cases, you will be able to replenish the bird's food and water from outside its quarters, but check that the pots cannot be dislodged by a bored parrot in search of a challenge. If you are in doubt, use a padlock for them as well. Once a parrot has mastered the knack of opening a door of any kind, it is likely to continue to do so, even if it leaves itself without food and water as a result.

REMOVABLE FLOORING

The other important thing to assess when looking at a flight cage is the ease with which it can be cleaned. Some cages are supplied with mesh grids above the floor area in order to stop the lining, such as sheets of newspaper, being disturbed and gnawed up by the parrot. In reality, however, droppings collect on the mesh, and so this has to be removed and scrubbed off. It can also represent a danger to the bird because it might end up with its foot stuck as it tries to walk over the floor area. It is therefore a good idea to remove a grid of this type from the outset. The tray itself should be heavy-duty. Check for dangerous gaps, particularly at the corners where the metal has been folded up at the sides to make a lip. It is quite possible for a bird to become trapped there and to slice its toe on the sharp edges of the metal. Finches and canaries are less vulnerable than parrots and mynah birds because their cages usually have plastic trays, but beware as there could be a large enough gap for them to escape through when the tray is removed for cleaning purposes.

◆ ABOVE LEFT
A large door opening provides good access to the interior of the cage, and this will make it easier to tame your bird.

◆ ABOVE RIGHT
Most parrot cages are provided with plastic containers, which can be used, as here, for food and water. A drinking bottle can also be used.

◆ LEFT
Ease of cleanliness is an important consideration in cage design. The lining tray of this flight cage can be easily removed for washing.

GARDEN AVIARIES

The design of a garden aviary will be influenced by the type of birds you wish to keep, and this in turn will have an impact on the cost of the aviary structure. Finches, for example, are relatively easy to accommodate as they are not destructive by nature, but they will need snug winter housing, and it would be beneficial to incorporate a birdroom into their aviary design. At the other extreme, large parrots can be very destructive and will need to be housed in steel rather than wooden-framed structures, with block-built shelters.

CHOOSING AN AVIARY

Scan the advertisement pages of the bird-keeping publications for details of aviary manufacturers and send for the catalogues. Be careful to compare like with like. Some firms offer simply the basic aviary, and charge extra for weatherproofing the timber, whereas in other cases, this is included in the total cost.

READY-MADE DESIGNS
Aviary manufacturers generally offer a range of their own designs as well as sectional units – mesh-clad flight panels, doors and similar units – from which you can construct a modular aviary to your own design. Before you buy, check the timber framework. Sometimes this is too thin and the mesh is not always securely attached to it. The framework should be made of wood which is at least 4 cm (1½ in) square, and proper netting staples should be used to attach the mesh. Ordinary staples will work loose over a period of time, creating gaps through which small birds may escape without difficulty. The situation may be exacerbated in a planted aviary by foliage growing up the mesh – its weight is likely to pull the wire off the framework if it is not firmly fixed in place. Netting staples should be driven in every 2.5–5 cm (1–2 in) around the frame to keep the mesh secure; regular checks on the mesh are essential.

It is quite easy to work out the number of panels you will need for an aviary, although it is worthwhile having your figures checked by the manufacturer before finalizing your order. Any discrepancies highlighted at this stage can be resolved easily, rather than when the structure is being assembled, by which time it will be too late.

Access to the structure will be influenced to a large extent by the layout of your garden. Try to disguise the entry point as far as possible, rather than placing it at the front of the flight, where it will be unattractive and make it harder to see the birds. A basic aviary design comprises a flight measuring 2.7 m (9 ft) long by 90 cm (3 ft) wide, attached to a shelter which is 90 cm (3 ft) square. For this design a single access point, at the back or on one side of the shelter, will be adequate. Entry to the flight, which is necessary for cleaning purposes and to catch the birds, is through a connecting door opening outwards from the shelter into this part of the aviary.

It is worthwhile incorporating a safety porch into the aviary design, to eliminate the risk of any birds escaping when you go in or out of the outer door into the flight. The safety porch allows you to enter the enclosed area and shut the door behind you before opening the aviary door. As a result, if a bird does happen to slip past you, it will remain within the confines of the safety porch, from where it can easily be returned to the aviary. A typical

♦ OPPOSITE LEFT
Not all aviaries have to be rectangular in shape.
This is an octagonal structure. Designs of this
type are available commercially from a number
of aviary suppliers.

♦ BELOW
A view from inside a service corridor, extending
along a block of metal-framed flights. This
design avoids the need for a safety porch and
makes it easier to attend to the birds' needs.

safety porch, measuring 90 cm (3 ft)
square, is constructed from wood
and mesh panels, like the flight
itself. Allow sufficient space, when
designing the aviary, for the safety
porch to open outwards. The door
into the aviary itself should be hinged
so that it swings into the flight. This
makes access easier, especially when
carrying cleaning tools, food pots or
the like. The safety porch can be
concealed, in the fullness of time, by
training evergreen climbing plants
up the wire frame.

MESH

The type of mesh used to cover the
aviary panels can have a significant
effect on the cost of the finished
structure. The cost rises significantly
as the strands become thicker. The
thickness of the strands is very
important – 19 gauge (19G) mesh
is quite suitable for smaller birds,
including finches, canaries, cockatiels
and budgerigars; thicker 16G is needed

for most parrots, including the Senegal
(*Poicephalus senegalus*), and 14G or
even 12G may be needed for the larger
cockatoos and macaws.

The separation distance of the
strands is also a vital consideration
to prevent escapes and safeguard the
birds' well-being. Most aviaries are
constructed using 2.5 x 1.25 cm (1 x
½ in) mesh, which is small enough to

exclude all but very young mice. Even
more secure is 1.25 cm (½ in) square
mesh, but this is rarely used by
aviary manufacturers because of the
increased cost. Small mesh makes it
much harder for large parrots to push
their bills between the strands and
obtain sufficient leverage to damage or
even cut through it; but the increased
cost means that generally a mesh
which is at least 2.5 cm (1 in) square
is used for their flights. It may be
cheaper to opt for 5 cm (2 in) square
mesh and cover this externally with
19G 2.5 x 1.25 cm (1 x ½ in) mesh to
exclude sparrows, snakes and rodents,
all of which can be hazardous in
different ways to aviary birds.

Most aviary designs are based on
90 cm (3 ft) units, simply because this
is the most commonly used width of
mesh rolls. Although wider rolls are
available, the mesh may tend to sag on
the framework of the flight, and this
will detract substantially from the
finished appearance of the aviary.

A view from inside an aviary showing a safety
porch in use. The purpose of the porch is to
stop birds escaping when you enter the aviary
by means of a double-doored entry system.

Doors must be hinged in such a way that they
give easy access to the interior of the aviary.
Once the structure is erected, it is difficult to
change the direction in which the doors open.

Over a period of time, and especially outdoors,
hinges may start to rust and seize up. It is
important to oil them at regular intervals
to prevent this from happening.

MAKING YOUR OWN AVIARY

In temperate areas, the best time to start building an aviary is in the spring, once the risk of frost has passed. You will be able to release the birds into their new home soon afterwards. Pairs may even breed that year, if they are already acclimatized to aviary life.

If you are building your own flight, it is best to use tanalized timber, i.e. timber that has been treated against rotting and has a long life expectancy. This is usually safe to use with livestock but, as always, check with your supplier if in doubt.

If, however, you are treating the timber yourself, ensure that the preservative you use will cause the birds no harm if they gnaw at it. The treated timber must be thoroughly dry before being assembled into frames and, as it is likely to require more than one coat, the whole process may take two or three weeks. Arrange to have the sections of timber cut to the

✦ ABOVE
It is worth examining ready-made display aviaries on site before deciding to build your own. This gives you the opportunity to consider various designs and to compare total costs.

✦ LEFT
Aviaries with boarding around the base are recommended for ground birds such as pheasants and quails, protecting them from dogs and cats, which could disturb them in the flight.

♦ BELOW
If you have space available, an aviary can be
incorporated alongside existing features in the
garden, such as this stone archway, with the
shelter being built out from the existing wall.

♦ BOTTOM
Blocks of aviaries are favoured for parrots and
parakeets. Because of the destructive nature of
these birds, it is not usually possible to add
plants to their enclosures.

appropriate lengths at the outset,
to save time and effort. It is better to
screw and preferably joint the timber
for the framework, rather than nailing
it together. The resulting frames are
less likely to twist, which may in turn
loosen the netting staples holding the
mesh in place. Remember to treat any
cut ends with a wood preservative
before assembly, because it is in such
areas that the timber is most likely to
start rotting.

An aviary is an expensive investment, but if well built at the outset
and carefully maintained, a timber
structure of this type should last for
well over 20 years. Buying the
cheapest materials can prove to be
false economy – rolls of aviary mesh
may look very similar, but the cheaper
unbranded rolls are unlikely to prove
as durable in the long term,
succumbing much more rapidly to
rust. This is harmful for parrots of all
types, because they climb over the
mesh and ingest particles which are
likely to cause irritation in their crops
or lower down in the digestive tract.

When it comes to attaching the
wire mesh to the frames, start by
placing the frames on a level surface.
It is a good idea to wear a pair of
gardening gloves when handling the
mesh. Be careful about cutting the
band around the roll because it is
likely to spring open at this point, and
could catch your face. Fix the cut end
in place, level with the top edge of the
flight frame, and unwind the roll,

taking care to keep it level and running
parallel with the sides of the frame.
It helps to have someone assisting
you with this task, so that you can tap
netting staples in while the mesh is
kept taut on the frame. If it runs
across at a slight angle, or is allowed
to hang loose, this will detract from
the appearance of the aviary once it is
finally assembled. At this preliminary
stage you can make slight adjustments
to tighten it as necessary, once it is
tacked in position.

You will need wire cutters to cut
off the mesh from the roll. Take care
to trim it so that loose ends, on which
the birds could injure themselves,
are cut right back to the nearest
horizontal strand at the top and
bottom of each panel. Finally, go
round and put in all the necessary
netting staples. Hardwood battening,
fixed over the edges of the mesh, will
keep the netting staples buried. Some
birds are likely to whittle away at this,
however, so check it regularly and be
prepared to replace it every so often,
once the aviary is occupied.

PREPARING THE SITE
FOR AN AVIARY

♦ BELOW
Just as in a garden it takes time for plants to
develop, the same applies in a planted aviary,
and results are likely to be seen more quickly
in a warm climate.

Before the aviary is ready to assemble
on site, mark out the area on the
ground where the structure is to be
located, using canes as a guide. Clear
the site as far as possible, carefully
removing any turf that you may want
to use in the aviary for landscaping
purposes. This can be cut out with a
sharp spade, rolled up and stored in
a shady spot until required. It is worth
clearing an additional area of turf from
around the perimeter, to be replaced
later, because the grass here will
inevitably be damaged during the
construction process.

The next stage is to mark out the
dimensions of the aviary accurately, so
that you can prepare the footings on
which the structure will rest. Secure
foundations are not only important
as an anchorage point; they also
prevent rodents, particularly rats,
from tunnelling into the birds'
quarters. Proper foundations prolong
the life of a wooden structure because
the timber is not in direct contact with
the ground, which can cause wood to
rot prematurely.

You will need to dig a trench
around the perimeter of the aviary
base to a depth of approximately
45 cm (18 in), using shuttering to
support the sides. Pour a thick layer
of concrete into the bottom of the
trench and allow it to set hard. This
is the foundation for the blockwork
walls. As the blocks are laid, check
that they are level, using a spirit level.
Above ground, you may prefer to use
bricks, which are more attractive than
blockwork. These should be laid in the
traditional way so that they overlap
from row to row, to give greater
strength to the finished structure.
The wall should extend approximately

30 cm (12 in) above the level of the
ground. Ideally, this work should be
carried out when the weather is fine
and it is unlikely to be frosty at night,
although there are products that can
be added to the mix to prevent it
deteriorating in the event of frost.
During hot weather, covering the
walls with damp sacking will prevent
the mortar drying too fast and
cracking as a result.

Decide on the floor covering at this
stage, while the area is fully accessible.
There are several options, depending
partly on the number and type of birds
you intend to house in the aviary.
Grass is often very appealing, but
unfortunately impractical. Drainage is
a major problem and often the grass
is replaced by moss. Where grass does
thrive, it soon becomes overgrown
and looks untidy; trying to cut it back
during the breeding season is not to be
recommended, because this disturbs
the birds. Maintaining an adequate
level of hygiene can also be a problem,
particularly if the aviary is home to
a relatively large number of birds.

The simplest solution is to opt for
a solid concrete base. This will add to
both the cost and work involved in
building the aviary, but in the long
term it will make it much easier to
keep the birds' surroundings clean.
Rain will help to wash away dirt from
the floor out of the aviary, and it can
be disinfected regularly. You will need
to incorporate a few small drainage
holes for this purpose at the opposite
end from the shelter. These openings
must not be large enough to allow
mice or snakes to gain access to the
aviary by this route. It is also important
to check them periodically to ensure
they are not blocked; if they are, the
aviary is likely to start flooding quite
rapidly when it rains hard.

For a concrete base, dig out the
floor to a depth of approximately
30 cm (12 in), pack the area with
hardcore and lay a 3:1 mix of ballast
and cement on top. Finally, lay a
smooth coat of mortar mixed with
sharp sand (very fine sand) on top,
to a depth of 15 cm (6 in). In the
shelter, thick plastic sheeting should

be laid between these two layers to act as a damp-proof course. It may be advisable to employ a bricklayer or plasterer to apply this final layer for you, in order to create a surface which slopes evenly down to the drainage points, with no areas where water will pool on the floor. Rapid drainage can help to prevent the development of unsightly green algae on the base as well, which could be dangerous as it may cause you to slip when you are moving around in the flight. This top layer can be applied only when the weather is sure to be fine; otherwise, it may be washed away before it sets.

A solid concrete base is especially valuable when you are housing a number of birds together because diseases can spread easily via soil contamination, and it is very difficult to eliminate harmful organisms once they have become established.

Parasitic worm eggs may survive in soil for more than two years, presenting a constant risk to birds foraging on the ground throughout this period.

Concrete presents problems if you decide to move house. The sectional design of aviaries means they can usually be dismantled and moved without any great difficulty, but this leaves the base, and prospective buyers may be put off by a large slab of concrete in the garden. One alternative, that provides the benefits of concrete without its permanence, is to use paving slabs for the floor. Make sure that they are slightly sloped for drainage. It is easy to move them along with the aviary, should you ever need to do so.

Another option, especially suitable for aviaries occupied by individual pairs of parakeets, is to spread a layer

of coarse gravel about 25 cm (10 in) thick on the floor of the aviary. Paving slabs can be set into the gravel beneath the perches, where the vast majority of droppings will accumulate. These can be easily scraped off with a small shovel, and the slabs can be thoroughly disinfected.

As an added precaution against rodents entering an aviary with a gravel base, cover the floor area with mesh, attaching this to the blockwork before tipping the gravel on top and setting the paving slabs in place.

By providing a good depth of gravel, not only will rain wash any dirt down between the stones, but there should be no risk of the birds having access to stale water before it drains away into the ground. A small drainage hole leading out of the flight at low level may be helpful as a further precaution.

◆ RIGHT
Where there are blocks of aviaries, it is important to be able to clean them easily. A concrete base, which can be hosed down from the outside, with the dirty water draining away along a gully, is often recommended.

ASSEMBLING THE AVIARY

This task requires two people. It helps to have all the sections identified with chalk, so that you can see how they fit together, and to arrange them on site accordingly. It is important to remember that in all cases, the wire-mesh face of the panel forms part of the interior of the flight. In the case of more destructive species, such as parakeets, this helps to protect the wooden framework from their bills.

Do not be tempted to fit the aviary doors at a preliminary stage – these should not be hung until the structure is in place; otherwise, they will be an obstruction. You will need bolts of the appropriate length to hold the wooden panels together, while frame-fixers can be used to anchor the frames down on to the base itself.

Start by fixing the end and one neighbouring side in place. The frames will be easier to support while you are working on them by being at right angles in this way. Stand them on a bed of concrete on top of the supporting wall for more anchorage. Do not forget to insert washers before the nuts, and oil them as well. This will make it easier to dismantle the aviary, should you need to move it. Oil the nuts every four to six months to prevent them from rusting and fusing on to the bolts. Thread the bolts through their fixing holes and tighten them in place.

Add the other side, and then the front of the shelter, which should be set on a course of bricks at the appropriate height. Fix on the sides of the shelter before finally adding the back. Fix the roof sections in place, on top of the assembled panels. Ensure that the roof of the flight is securely fixed to the sides.

ASSEMBLING THE AVIARY

TURF REMOVED FROM THE DUGOUT AREA

DUGOUT AREA FOR FOOTINGS

1 Preparing the site and footings to support the aviary is important, both to ensure the stability of the aviary, and also to exclude rodents. You may need to use shuttering to hold back the soil when you are digging out the base. Keep turf from the dug out area to be refitted later around the outside.

2 Blocks can be laid below ground level, but brickwork will create a more attractive appearance above the soil. It is vital to ensure the course of bricks overlaps, because it is this that will make the structure secure. It may be necessary to recruit the help of a professional bricklayer at this stage.

PANEL TO PROVIDE SHADE AND PROTECTION

TIMBER BATONS FOR MOUNTING FRAMES

BRICKS OR BLOCKS

3 The actual design of aviaries can differ significantly. The back panel in this case helps to provide additional protection for small non-destructive birds, such as finches and the smaller softbills. Note the space provided here for the safety porch.

The roof of the shelter can be built to form an apex, but it will be much simpler to have a roof section which slopes down away from the flight. Cover it with two layers of a good-quality roofing felt. Tuck these firmly down at the sides, to lessen the risk of the felt being torn off in strong winds.

The interior needs to be well lit in order to attract the birds into this part of the aviary, so it should have an opaque glass window. Avoid clear glass

4 The sections of the aviary should be bolted together. Do not fit the doors in place until everything is assembled on the base, because it will be harder to manipulate the panels. Because of the size of the structure, assembling the aviary is a task for two people.

– the birds will not see it and may attempt to fly through what they see as an opening, injuring or even killing themselves. If for some reason clear glass is unavoidable, this must be adequately screened with mesh.

Fit the door of the shelter once everything else is in place. Select robust hinges. It will save you time and money in the long run to spend a little more at this stage. It is a nuisance to be faced with a door that sticks because the hinges have started to rust within a few months of setting up the aviary. Keep the hardware well oiled, however much you spend. This applies equally to the door lock, which should, if possible, be an integral part of the structure so as to offer more security. The number of thefts of aviary birds has increased over recent years, and every effort should be made to deter casual thieves from gaining access to the aviary, especially as once stolen, birds are rarely recovered.

5 The safety porch should blend in as far as possible, rather than detracting from the aviary's appearance. If the translucent plastic sheeting applied over the mesh on the roof is linked with guttering, rain water can be channelled off to a water-butt.

6 *(right)* Security is an important feature of aviary design. Fitting a combination lock to the outside door will mean you do not need to worry about carrying keys each time you visit the birds. A bolt should be fitted on the inside of both doors, so that you can close them securely as you enter the aviary.

FINISHING OFF

Even if you buy a complete aviary, you will probably need to invest in some corrugated plastic sheeting and guttering. The sheeting should be fixed on the flight roof nearest to the shelter, using the special fitments available for this purpose. It will provide protection for the birds when they are in the flight, and should be extended down the sides. Use a wooden framework to slope the plastic sheeting away from the shelter, and fix guttering at the lower edge to prevent rainwater from pouring into the flight itself. Guttering will also be needed at the lowest edge of the shelter roof. The down pipe can be connected to a water butt, to provide water for the garden.

Perches in the aviary should always be arranged across the flight, but do not clutter the area, so the birds can benefit from the flying space. Have two main perches at either end of the flight, one located under cover. Make

♦ A B O V E
Devise your planting scheme at the outset. Include plants which will give the birds cover for nesting purposes, and will attract insects.

♦ B E L O W
Climbing plants and hanging baskets can be used outside the aviary, but ensure these will not damage the structure in any way.

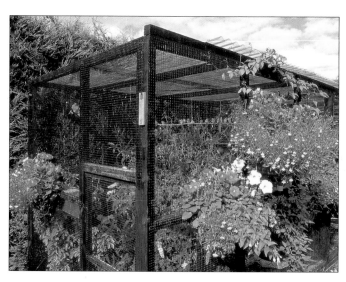

sure that this one does not block the connecting door leading from the shelter to the flight. Allow sufficient space for the birds to move freely on the perches, with no risk of rubbing their tails on the mesh at the far end.

It is not a good idea to force the perches up against the wire mesh because after a while, with the constant friction caused by the birds moving on and off the perch, the mesh will be weakened, holes will develop in it and the perch is likely to collapse. It is much better to arrange the perches so that they can be supported by the wooden uprights in the flight.

Another possibility is to set perches in a container. A crown of branches is especially good for this purpose. For larger parrots, which need relatively strong perches to carry their weight, it may be better to fix these on a length of timber approximately 5 cm (2 in) square, which can be set into a pre-formed hole in the aviary floor. It is easy to replace such perches when they are destroyed, by knocking off the branch from the wooden support and fixing a new one in place.

Many birds, particularly finches and softbills, benefit from being kept in an enclosure with growing plants. These not only provide cover, which can be vital for nesting purposes, but also attract insects, which will help to supplement the birds' diet. Suitable shrubs, such as conifers, can be introduced to the flight in tubs, while ground cover can be provided by means of annuals, such as nasturtiums (*Tropaeolum majus*).

It is important to landscape the aviary into the garden once building work is complete. You may decide to have a flowerbed around the base of the aviary for example, and you can soften the outlines of the shelter by growing a climbing plant up the sides. Replant some of the turf, and set a row of paving stones around the perimeter of the aviary to give easy access to the safety porch off an existing path.

♦ ABOVE
If building a pond in your aviary, make sure there is a shallow area at one end: smaller birds in the aviary can easily fall in and drown.

♦ BELOW
Even alongside bare aviaries, flower beds can be included to create colour and a changing focus of interest through the seasons.

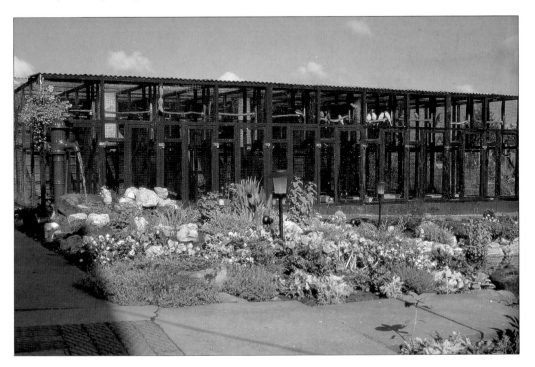

BIRDROOMS

◆ BELOW
A birdroom in the form of a garden shed. Wire
frames must be placed over windows to prevent
birds escaping or injuring themselves on glass.

Although the basic aviary design will
be adequate in many cases, it can be
helpful to have a birdroom as well,
particularly if you are interested in
keeping the more delicate species,
including various finches and softbills,
which require warm indoor housing
in winter, or are keen to exhibit your
birds. The additional space provided
by a birdroom will be invaluable in
either case.

As its name suggests, a birdroom
is an indoor area where birds are
housed. If at all possible, purchase an
integrated birdroom and aviary at the
outset. Often, the birdroom structure
will connect with the aviary flight
and will include the shelter; this is the
most convenient set-up. You could
adapt a large existing garden shed to
use as a birdroom, although this may
mean having two separate buildings,
and you will be constantly moving
back and forth between them,
sometimes carrying birds.

◆ BELOW
In a large set-up, birdrooms provide space for
indoor flights, breeding cages and food storage.

In an integrated set-up, the aviary
shelter forms part of the birdroom,
usually occupying the far end of the
structure. This allows for breeding
or stock cages to be positioned down
one side, while there may be an indoor
flight opposite. There is also space
for the storage of foodstuffs and
other equipment, such as nest boxes
and extra food and drink containers.

During the winter in temperate
areas, the interior can be heated by
means of a thermostatically controlled
tubular heater. Heating costs can be
drastically reduced by fitting draught
excluders around the doors and
windows, as well as fitting insulation
material into the walls of the
birdroom. This can be placed behind
plywood or even hardboard, but
beware of rodents; they can establish
themselves rapidly in such warm and
comfortable surroundings.

The strength of wire mesh depends partly on its gauge size. This is 19 gauge (19G), the thinnest mesh used in aviary construction.

Although the strand dimensions are the same 2.5 x 1.25 cm (1 x ½ in) this sample of mesh is 16G, which is heavier than 19G.

Plastic coated mesh is suitable for finches and softbills but not for parrots, which may nibble off the protective coating.

Artificial lighting can also be fitted in a birdroom, extending the feeding period when days are at their darkest. It is possible to operate birdroom lighting automatically, using either a time switch or a light sensor. Incorporating a dimming control in the circuitry allows birds to find their way back to the perches if they are feeding when the lights go off, rather than plunging them into sudden darkness. Restrict their light exposure to no more than about 12 hours in total each day or you could start interfering with the breeding cycle.

Some birds, particularly finches and some parrots, can generate large amounts of feather dust, and this in turn may cause allergic reactions, particularly in people susceptible to asthma. Although good hygiene will minimize the problem, incorporating an ionizer into the birdroom can reduce the particles in the atmosphere. A constant stream of billions of electrons is released from the tip of the ionizer, and when these collide with a dust particle, the particle falls down on to an earthed surface from where it can be wiped away with a damp kitchen towel. Another advantage of having an ionizer in a birdroom is that it destroys potentially harmful microbes, such as the virus responsible for French moult.

A tubular convector heater should be shielded in a metal cage to prevent birds gnawing the electrical connections or burning themselves.

An ionizer will improve the environment within a birdroom by removing dust and germs from the air.

Additional lighting can be very valuable in a birdroom, particularly in temperate areas, allowing the birds' feeding period to be extended on dull days. Fluorescent strip lights give off a more natural light, although they cannot be operated with a conventional dimmer switch.

HOUSING CHOICES

A number of different housing options are available, when it comes to accommodating birds in outdoor quarters, but you may need to adapt a standard aviary to meet the needs of the birds which you want to keep. This might entail cutting a pop-hole at ground level, through the door connecting the flight and shelter, to give easy access to quails living in the aviary. Alternatively, it could be a matter of running wire strands on vertical uprights around the edge of the entire roof of the aviary, with a view to stopping cats from climbing up here and disturbing the birds. If you are having the aviary built for you, most manufacturers will be happy to incorporate such personal refinements during the construction process, at a cost which needs to be agreed in advance. You can then simply concentrate on the finishing touches – fitting out the aviary with perches and plants to meet the birds' needs.

♦ TOP
A concrete base is easily cleaned and disinfected at intervals as required, preventing a build-up of parasites such as intestinal worms in the birds' environment.

♦ ABOVE LEFT
Food such as seed husks will often end up scattered by the birds outside indoor quarters, so it helps to ensure that the surrounding area can be cleaned easily. Castors will allow the cage to be moved for cleaning purposes.

♦ ABOVE RIGHT
When a group of birds such as budgerigars are housed together, the perches often become dirty. These should be removable, if possible, so they can be scrubbed clean on a regular basis.

♦ LEFT
Good ventilation in birdrooms is important to prevent a build-up of stale air, which could be harmful. Separate housing to accommodate new birds for the first few weeks will help safeguard the health of established bird stock.

HOUSING CHOICES

Finches: these relatively small birds are generally kept in planted aviaries, either in a colony or as part of a mixed collection. In temperate areas, they require heated wintertime accommodation, with extra lighting to extend the feeding time.

Softbills: size is often quite a good indicator of their relative hardiness. The more delicate species will be most at home in a snug conservatory-type aviary, which is well protected, but others are quite hardy, with the larger species thriving in large aviaries. Ease of cleaning is an important design consideration.

Parakeets: while some parakeets, such as the budgerigar, can be kept in a colony, the majority need to be accommodated in individual pairs. Their aviaries can be arranged in blocks, provided the sides of adjoining flights are double-wired.

Larger parrots: if timber is used in the construction of the flights for these birds, it must be well protected from their powerful bills. The mesh, too, must be suitably robust. A brick-built shelter offers a more durable option than a wooden structure, with a metal framework being used for the aviary panels. These can be obtained from specialist aviary manufacturers.

Pheasants and quails: pheasants in particular require spacious flights, and are often housed in the company of larger softbills, such as touracos. They spend much of their time on the floor of their flight, so a well-drained base is essential. There must be vegetation to provide them with cover, preferably with areas of grass, and gravel should be available, spread around the perimeter of the flight.

✦ TOP RIGHT
Some birds, such as quails and pheasants, appreciate more seclusion in their quarters than others, like Australian parakeets. Adapt housing to the birds' needs wherever possible.

✦ ABOVE RIGHT
Secure door fastenings are very important on aviaries, especially those situated at a distance from the house. A lock built into the door will help to deter potential vandals and thieves.

✦ BELOW
A block of raised aviaries intended for parrots and parakeets. The birds are fed at the back of the structure, and the raised floor area will usually have a mesh base.

✦ ABOVE
The aviary framework can be securely attached to an aviary wall, and this will create a snug environment, especially for smaller birds. Making birds more comfortable in their home will help them to settle down quickly.

FOODS AND THEIR USES

The nutritional needs of pet birds are better understood now than in the past, and it is easier than ever to feed them well. Seed mixes are available from pet stores, along with an increasing range of complete diets, which provide not just the essential carbohydrates, fats and proteins, but also the vitamins and minerals which are equally important to a bird's well-being. Unfortunately, however, not all birds take to complete diets straight away. Much depends on the bird's background – hand-reared parrots are more likely to sample unfamiliar foods than birds that have been fed on seed for most of their lives.

Softbills and nectar-feeders have the most specialized feeding habits. You may need to buy some foods by mail-order, and the preparation is more time-consuming than for seed-eaters.

Better nutrition results in better breeding, particularly in the case of parrots. It is not a coincidence that those birds adapted to feed and breed on fairly meagre rations, such as the budgerigar and other Australian species, were the first to reproduce readily in captivity. Today, however, almost any parrot can be expected to breed in suitable surroundings, if provided with a varied and nutritious diet.

◆ OPPOSITE
Cockatiels rank among the easiest birds
to feed, as they will subsist mainly on seed,
although a wide selection of greenstuff
should also be provided.

◆ LEFT
Fruit plays an important part in the diet
of many birds, particularly softbills and
parrots. The way in which the food is
prepared depends on the feeding habits
of the individual species.

FEEDING SEED-EATERS

Parrots and finches are generally classed as seed-eaters to distinguish them from the softbills, which are not fed significant amounts of seed. The seeds used as bird food can be broadly divided into two categories, based on their nutritional values. There are the oil seeds, characterized by relatively high fat content, and the cereals, the main chemical constituent of which is carbohydrate.

OIL SEEDS

These form the basis of seed mixtures for parrots. The major ingredient is usually the widely available striped sunflower seed, with its blackish and white stripes. Other forms of sunflower seed may also be included; black sunflower has a smaller, plumper seed than the striped, as does white sunflower. White sunflower seed is sometimes confused with another ingredient of some parrot mixes, safflower seed, although this is plumper and more angular. In nutritional terms, white sunflower is generally the best option for bird food because it has a lower oil content, but the yield from these seedheads is lower than from the striped form, and so the price is slightly higher.

Peanuts are another typical oil seed included in most parrot mixes. They can be purchased still in their flaky shells as groundnuts, but buying them in this state means that they are correspondingly expensive because the parrots discard the casing. For the same reason, it is usually not worth choosing the larger grades of sunflower seed – in most cases, the kernel within is no larger than in small seeds, so you are paying for wastage. Peanuts can be dangerous, because it

is very difficult to spot contamination. The harmful *Aspergillus* mould can be detected only by testing, and for this reason it is important to buy peanuts from reputable suppliers who can guarantee the quality of their seed. Unfortunately, the effects of the toxins produced by this fungus are

FOOD FOR SEED-EATERS

Oil seeds:	Cereals:
Blue maw	Canary seed
Hemp	Groats
Linseed	Maize (corn)
Niger seed	Millet
Peanuts	Paddy rice
Perilla seed	
Pine nuts	
Pumpkin seed	
Rape seed	
Safflower seed	
Sunflower seed	
Teasel seed	

not immediately apparent, and they can result in long-term liver damage.

Not all the seeds included in parrot mixes are grown commercially. Some are still gathered from the wild, notably pine nuts, which are collected in the vast coniferous forests of the former Soviet Union and China. The larger nuts are suitable for most parrots, and the small nuts are valuable for larger finches as well. Always check the nuts carefully for signs of any obvious fungal contamination, which can give rise to a bluish growth on chipped nuts. These could be harmful to the birds.

Smaller oil seeds feature prominently in seed mixtures for canaries. Red rape is an important ingredient, although other types of rape seed are also used. Black rape is particularly valued as soaked seed, while German rubsen rape is favoured by keepers of roller canaries because it is believed to enhance the birds' singing abilities.

Hemp is probably the most popular seed with canaries themselves, and they will frequently scatter the contents of their food container, seeking it out. A round, darkish seed, hemp is also included in parrot seed mixes but it should be used sparingly, and not just because of its high oil content. It can actually alter the appearance of some birds, giving rise to the phenomenon described as "acquired melanism". This causes lighter-coloured areas of the plumage, such as the red chest of a bullfinch (*Pyrrhula pyrrhula*), to turn black. The effect is not permanent, but it will last until the next moult when the plumage is replaced, assuming that the bird's diet is corrected before then.

A variety of other oil seeds are used as bird food, often in larger amounts

◆ LEFT
Many bird-keepers buy seed mixes, which contain a variety of different seeds, rather than preparing their own mixes. This is a typical parrot seed mix. As a rule, the more expensive mixes will usually have a wider range of ingredients.

at certain times of the year. Niger, for example, with its unmistakable elongated blackish shape, is considered valuable to protect against egg-binding, and is fed primarily before the start of the canary breeding season. Teasel seed is expensive but

highly valued by breeders as a rearing food for canaries and similar species, such as serins. Once the chicks are ready to be weaned, blue maw is often sprinkled on top of their softfood to encourage them to start eating seed on their own, its small size being ideal for this purpose.

New seeds are regularly added to the list of those used as bird food. In recent years, perilla has become favoured as a tonic seed, and is used when birds are moulting or recuperating from illness. Pumpkin seeds are now widely used for parrots, providing a valuable source of the antioxidant Vitamin E.

Linseed

Pine nuts

Pumpkin seeds

Safflower seeds

Sunflower seeds

◆ **BOTTOM**
It is possible to provide food in open pots, which will fix on to the cage front. There is likely to be more wastage, however, as the bird will scatter seed on the floor.

◆ **BELOW**
Seed hoppers come in various designs, suitable for different birds, such as these Norwich canaries. All provide a reservoir of seed, which is kept free from the birds' droppings.

CEREALS

The term "canary seed" can be confusing, because it can refer to either a mixture or an individual seed, often called a "straight" in the trade, to distinguish it from a mix. Plain canary seed is widely grown as bird food in a range of countries, including Australia, Canada and Morocco, with smaller amounts being cultivated commercially in other countries, including England. It is a relatively small, light-brownish seed with a dark covering to the kernel inside, and is oval in shape with pointed ends. Aside from featuring significantly in canary seed mixes, it is also an important ingredient of blends of budgerigar seed and is included, to a lesser extent, in the diets of finches.

Millet is the other major cereal seed used in bird food for a wide range of species. A number of distinctive forms of millets are available, often sold on the basis of their colour, such as red, yellow and pearl white millets. The most popular variety tends to be panicum, which is sold in seedhead form as millet sprays. Millet is a valuable rearing food, often being provided in a soaked form when there are chicks in the nest. The larger, harder millets such as pearl white are most suitable for budgerigars, cockatiels and parakeets, rather than small finches, which may encounter difficulties in cracking the seeds.

Groats, which are the dehulled form of oats, are sometimes added to seed mixtures, as well as being used by budgerigar breeders to feed breeding stock. Groats can be fattening, however, particularly for birds housed in breeding cages, and the amount offered should be restricted accordingly.

While most parrot mixtures contain little in the way of cereal seeds, they may incorporate kibbled maize (corn), i.e. broken maize. Whole maize is a very hard seed once it has been dried, and only the largest parrots have bills strong enough to crack it. Flaked maize, which looks something like cornflakes, is included in some mixes.

Some mixtures include paddy rice. This is a relatively flat, yellowish seed that may be eaten by small parrots and large finches such as Java sparrows, which are also known as rice birds (*Padda oryzivora*).

Pheasants and quails may be fed on cereals of various types; special mixes are available for them from larger pet stores and bird seed suppliers; these will ensure they receive the correct nutritional balance. Pellets sometimes feature in their diets.

PREPARING SEED

Over recent years, there has been a growing appreciation of the fact that in the wild, virtually no birds feed predominantly on dry seed, and that birds can gain considerable benefits from being fed either soaked or sprouted seeds. Many of the pulses, such as mung beans, which are popular for human consumption are now often used as bird food, especially for parrots, along with more conventional seeds such as millets and canary seed.

Start by washing the required quantity of seed in a sieve under running water to remove any dust that may have accumulated during storage. Then tip the rinsed seed into a heatproof container, cover with hot water, and leave to stand overnight. Such treatment triggers the germination process, causing the protein levels in the seed to rise, and increasing the level of Vitamin B. The seed also changes in texture when saturated, becoming softer and more digestible. Soaked seed is especially valued during the breeding period, when there are chicks in the nest. It can also prove to be a lifesaver for sick

Self-sown canary seed

or weak birds, especially small finches; they may not have the strength to crack the dry seed, but can often be persuaded to sample a soaked millet spray, which will significantly improve their chances of recovery.

After being left to stand, soaked seed must always be washed again, very thoroughly, before being fed to the birds. It will now be perishable, so that any seed left uneaten at the end of the day must be removed and disposed of before it becomes contaminated with moulds. This is especially likely during hot weather.

The same applies in the case of sprouted seed, which is prepared in the same way as for human consumption, washing off the sprouts thoroughly in fresh water before offering them to the birds. You will soon be able to gauge the amount of seed required by your birds, to avoid unnecessary wastage.

Chick-peas

Oats

Japanese millet

Mung beans

Hemp

Panicum millet

BUYING SEEDS

Where you obtain seed will depend on the type and number of birds you are keeping. If you have a pet budgerigar, the simplest solution is to buy a packeted seed mix from a local pet store. If you have a large collection of birds, it may be more convenient to find a mail-order supplier who will arrange delivery direct to your door. Most pet stores can offer mixtures to suit different types of birds, but they may not be able to offer you straights such as teasel or perilla. These will have to be obtained through a more specialist bird feed supplier. Look through the advertisements in the bird-keeping publications.

From a pet store, buy seed that is bagged or packeted rather than loose, especially if birds are kept in the store. The viruses responsible for French moult and psittacine beak and feather disease (PBFD) can be spread easily via feather dust, and may also contaminate any nearby seed supplies.

There is also a risk from rodents. Any seed which is soiled with their droppings or urine is a potential health hazard to all birds and must be discarded. Storing seed in metal bins helps to exclude rodents from gaining access to it. Unfortunately, buying seed from bins gives you no idea of its freshness. It may be that new seed is being tipped on top of old, rather than the bin being properly emptied before the new seed is added. An advantage of purchasing from one of the main seed suppliers is that they are likely to have a higher stock turnover than a pet store, and their supplies should be relatively fresh.

Bird seed will not deteriorate rapidly, provided that it is kept dry, but try to rotate stocks so that you have no more than about four months' supply on hand at any stage. This will also decrease the likelihood of contamination by fodder mites. These tiny creatures are barely visible to the naked eye, but they impart a characteristically sweet odour to the seed. Sniff a handful to check. Whether fodder mites harm the birds directly is unclear, but they will certainly not improve the nutritional value of the seed.

Most seed now is clean, containing little or no obvious traces of dust or harvesting debris, thanks to computer-controlled cleaning processes, but if you are offered dirty seed by a supplier, do not hesitate to reject it.

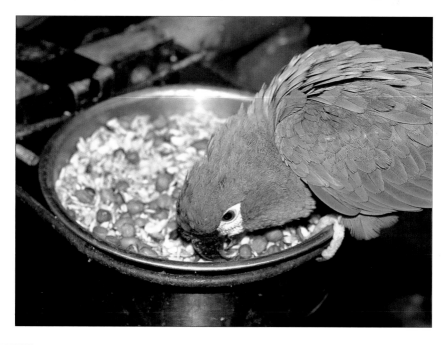

♦ LEFT
A range of foods will be eaten by parrots. Do not provide these birds primarily with dry seed. This is nutritionally unbalanced, lacking certain vital vitamins and minerals.

GRIT AND CUTTLEFISH

Seed-eating birds often consume grit – small pieces of stone that accumulate in the bird's gizzard. Grit helps the bird to grind up seeds by the muscular action of the gizzard walls, and it contributes valuable minerals. Two types of grit are sold to bird-keepers and they differ in their chemical properties. Oyster shell grit is soluble, and it breaks down in the acid medium of the gizzard, allowing the minerals to be absorbed by the body; mineralized grit is insoluble, remaining for a longer time in the gizzard. Grit should always be available to seed-eating species, although consumption may be variable. The grit container should be topped up regularly with fresh grit to ensure that the birds have a good supply of particles of a suitable size.

Cuttlefish bone is important as a source of minerals, especially calcium which is lacking in seed. Just prior to the breeding season, hens will often

spend much longer at the cuttlefish bone, nibbling away at it to build up their body calcium stores for the egg-laying period ahead. The soft powdery side should always be accessible to

Iodine nibble

them. For finches, it is a good idea to cut off some slivers with a sharp knife, making it easier for the birds to nibble at the surface.

An iodine nibble is recommended, especially for budgerigars. These parakeets seem to have a particular requirement for this trace element: any deficiency will slow the moulting process. If you have exhibition birds, it may be better to provide white iodine nibbles rather than the more traditional pink variety, which could stain the facial feathering just prior to a show.

Oyster shell

Kilpatricks salts

Limestone

Grit mix

Mineralized grit

Egg food

A BALANCED DIET

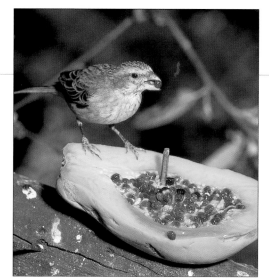

♦ LEFT
It is not unusual for seed-eaters to take a wider range of food than they might otherwise be offered. Do not be afraid to experiment within reason. Birds, like ourselves, have individual tastes.

No bird should be expected to subsist entirely on a diet of dry seeds. Seeds are low in essential amino acids, which are the key components of protein, and also in vitamins and minerals, such as Vitamin A and calcium. Birds require a much wider range of foodstuffs to fulfil all their nutritional needs.

If your bird refuses to take a complete diet, you will have to rely on supplements to compensate for dietary shortcomings. These are available in both liquid and powdered forms. Liquid preparations should be added in the correct proportion to the birds' drinking water. They tend to be less comprehensive in terms of their ingredients than powdered supplements, and there is no guarantee that the birds will drink sufficient water to gain maximum benefit,

particularly if the weather is wet, when they may prefer to drink raindrops off the mesh.

Powdered supplements should be sprinkled over greenstuff or fruit. They will not adhere well to dry seed, simply sinking to the bottom of the

food container. A variety of greenstuff is readily taken by many species ranging from parrots to pheasants. Most softbills prefer fruit, but touracos will consume large quantities of greenstuff as part of their regular diet. Aim to provide regular amounts

Parakeet mix

Parakeet mix and fruit

Pheasant mix

Pigeon and dove seed

Foreign finch seed mix

Aviary mix

Greenstuff can be used to encourage a pet bird, such as this cockatiel, to feed from your hand. Always wash greenstuff and fruit thoroughly before offering it to birds.

GREENSTUFF AND FRUIT FOR SEED-EATERS

Use these:	Avoid these:
Chickweed	Avocado
Dandelion	Citrus fruits
Seeding	Bananas
grasses	
Spinach beet	
Brassicas	
Carrots	
Sweet apples	
Grapes	
Pomegranates	

of whatever is available, rather than large quantities occasionally, which can lead to digestive upsets if the birds gorge themselves.

Among wild plants, chickweed, dandelion and seeding grass are all likely to be eaten, but do not collect them from areas where they may have been sprayed with herbicides, such as roadside verges. In terms of cultivated vegetables, spinach beet can be grown easily and will provide a source of greenstuff even through the winter, as may brassicas such as broccoli.

Carrots, too, can be valuable, especially as they contain a precursor of Vitamin A. They should be peeled and cut into small pieces to prevent wastage; some larger parrots can be reluctant to descend to

the floor of their quarters if they drop their food, and they are less likely to drop the smaller chunks.

One fruit which should never be given to birds is avocado, because this may be poisonous for them. It is generally better to avoid citrus fruits because their acidic nature can lead to scouring. Bananas are not generally recommended because they can be messy and may stain the plumage around the bill. Any unripe fruit can be indigestible.

Pomegranate

Sweet apples are widely used, and grapes are a popular choice, although they contain relatively little in the way of nutrients.

In some cases, with mynah birds for example, you will need to dice the fruit into small pieces which the birds can swallow whole, whereas for other birds, including parrots, you can provide the fruit in chunks. A favourite fruit with parrots is pomegranates, which can be stored in a cool, dry place for a month or more, extending their availability after the end of the season. In tropical regions, a wider range of fruits is available, but try to select fruits which are firm and not especially juicy. The juice may stain the birds' plumage and this can attract insects such as wasps.

Apples

Grapes

Carrots

FEEDING NECTAR MIXES

Within the parrot family, the lories and lorikeets have adapted to feed naturally on nectar and pollen. Special tiny brushes on the tongue sweep the pollen granules into the mouth so they can be swallowed easily. Whereas pollen is a valuable source of protein, the carbohydrate content of the diet comes from the nectar itself, which consists of various sugars.

In the past, bird-keepers were forced to rely on home-made nectar mixtures using ingredients such as honey, which would often attract bees to the drinker. The birds were therefore in danger of being stung when they fed. Today, a good range of proprietary nectar mixtures is available, generally in powdered form. They simply need to be mixed with water. The mixtures are supplemented with vitamins and minerals and

contain all the necessary ingredients to keep birds in the best of health.

There are several different types available for the various groups of nectivores. Besides those suitable for lories, lorikeets and hanging parrots, there are specific mixtures formulated for hummingbirds and other small nectivores, such as sugarbirds, sunbirds and white-eyes. Do not be tempted to change brands suddenly, particularly when acquiring a new bird. Instead, stick to its established diet, offering the new food in increasing amounts over a fortnight or so. This should avoid causing any digestive upsets, which may prove to be fatal in this group of birds. Nectar foods are not as widely available as seed – you will probably need to obtain them from a bird farm or specialist avian supplier.

♦ LEFT AND ABOVE
All nectar drinking equipment has a red spout, since studies have shown that this is the colour which is most likely to attract birds such as this hummingbird to feed. Tinted glass on the drinker will help to protect the vitamin value of the food.

Lory mix nectar and fruit

Lory mix

FEEDING SOFTBILLS

Finches will eat a wider range of food than dry
seed, and a varied diet is beneficial for them.
Softfood, shown here, can be an important
rearing food when there are chicks in the nest.

A number of different brands of
softbill foods are available. There are
general softbill diets, and it is also
possible to obtain more specialist
foods, catering for either insectivorous
or frugivorous species. In most cases,
softbill food is sprinkled over fruit,
to which it adheres well. Choose one
of the low-iron brands; the birds that
tend to be the most frugivorous in
their feeding habits, such as tanagers,
barbets and toucans, as well as
mynahs, are especially vulnerable to
iron storage disease. This condition,
caused by a build-up of iron in the
liver, is very hard to treat and usually
proves fatal. These birds have a highly
efficient iron absorption mechanism in
their intestines, and lowering the level
of iron in their diet is the best way of
protecting them from the illness.
Dried fruits should also be used in
moderation for this reason.

Softbill pellets are available,
including low-iron brands. Pellets are
ideal for mynahs and touracos. The

Softbill mix

birds eat them rather like berries. You
may need to soak the pellets in a cup
of water beforehand in order to soften
them and make them more palatable.

Food needs to be prepared fresh on
a daily basis because it will soon start
to deteriorate, particularly in hot
weather, and this could endanger the
birds' health. Do not be tempted to
use ingredients which are past their
recommended "use by" date; the
vitamin content may have declined,
and this can lead to a deficiency.

◆ LEFT AND RIGHT
Always prepare bird foods
in clean surroundings,
cutting up the fruit to meet
the birds' individual needs.

LIVEFOODS

Many birds rely on livefood in their
diet to a greater or lesser extent,
particularly during the breeding
season. Some softbills must be offered
livefood on a regular basis, whereas
the majority of parrots will not eat
invertebrates at all. In the past, bird-
keepers had either to forage for
livefood themselves, or breed their
own; today, the supply of livefoods has
developed into a huge business
worldwide. It is much safer to rely on
those that are commercially available
because you can be sure that they are
free from the parasites that can afflict
wild invertebrates, and spread to birds
when they consume them.

The two most widely used forms of
livefood are mealworms, which are the
larval stage of the meal beetle
(*Tenebrio molitor*), and crickets. You

can buy them in a variety of sizes to
suit all birds. These invertebrates do
not have a good calcium:phosphorus
ratio, so if birds eat them as the main
part of their diet, they may develop
calcium deficiency. In order to combat
this, the technique known as "gut
loading" has become popular. The
mealworms and crickets are given
special foods so that the bird, when it

eats them, will benefit from the food
still present in their gut.

There are also special nutritional
"balancers" which serve to correct the
deficiencies in livefoods, and are easy
to use. The invertebrates are
transferred to a plastic bag and
powder is tipped over them before
they are offered to the birds. Some of
the powder will be swallowed by the

bird when it catches the invertebrate
in due course. In order to slow down
crickets, and so make it easier for birds
to catch them, you can put them in the
fridge, in a suitable container, for half
an hour or so before feeding time.

Micro-crickets can be offered to
waxbills when they are rearing their
chicks, as well as to softbills of similar
size, while large crickets are suitable

Waxworm larvae

Mealworms

for birds such as laughing thrushes. Livefoods can be a useful aid if you are trying to tame birds in aviary surroundings. Before long, you are likely to find that a pair will come to recognize the livefood container, and may even be persuaded to feed from your hand.

Among other livefoods to choose from are waxworms, which are the larval waxmoths, and redworms, popular with larger softbills.

In most cases, breeding livefoods at home is unlikely to be worth the effort, partly because, as in the case of mealworms, the life cycle takes several months to complete. The mealworms turn into immobile pupae before hatching into blackish beetles and laying the eggs, which will ultimately hatch into more tiny mealworms.

However, two important types of livefoods, whiteworms and fruit flies, are available only in the form of starter cultures, which means that if you want to offer these to your birds, you will have to breed them yourself.

Whiteworms and similar tiny worms, such as microworms, need to be kept damp. Bury the starter culture with some bread, soaked in milk, just under the surface of peat, or a similar substrate, in a lidded plastic tub. The lid should have several small holes punched in it for ventilation. Top up the food supply as necessary. If left in a relatively warm spot, and not allowed to dry out, the worms can be harvested a month or so later. Simply spoon the substrate with the worm colony into a saucer of water and catch the worms with a fine tea-strainer.

Setting up several cultures in succession will guarantee a plentiful supply of these invertebrates throughout the breeding season.

Fruit flies are taken by hummingbirds and other smaller nectivores. Place a layer of the starter culture in the bottom of the special container supplied with it, where the flies can lay their eggs. Alternatively, a large glass jar covered with muslin (cheesecloth) and containing a banana skin should provide the appropriate climate to establish a culture, which needs to be warm. It may help to start out with the wingless strain of fruit flies, as they will be easier for the birds to catch. To feed the flies, simply cut a hole in the muslin; the flies will find their own way out, and the birds will catch them easily.

♦ BELOW
Mealworms will ultimately metamorphose into adult meal beetles, but keeping them relatively cool will slow this change. They first turn into pupae, becoming inactive at this stage.

COLOUR FOODS AND THE MOULT

It was back in the 1870s that an accidental discovery revolutionized the care of canary birds, when a breeder gave some cayenne pepper as a tonic to an ailing bird which was moulting. This canary not only survived, but the breeder was amazed to see how the colour of its new plumage was transformed into a much brighter shade than previously. In due course, this canary shone on the show bench, and breeders sought the secret of how the bird's plumage had become so magnificently coloured.

The secret soon leaked out, and before long, colour-feeding, as this practice is known, became widely-accepted for show purposes in the case of many canary breeds. During the early days, the emphasis was placed on natural ingredients which could exert the colour effect, but today, synthetic derivatives are much

♦ RIGHT
The effects of colour feeding are seen here in the richer tone of this canary's emerging feathers.

♦ BELOW
Colour food for birds is available either in the form of a softfood, or as a liquid.

♦ RIGHT
An unflighted canary. The description "unflighted" refers to the pale flight and tail feathers in this young bird.

more commonly used. These are available either in the form of liquids, which need to be added to the bird's drinking water, or alternatively, as colour food added to softfood.

The timing of colour feeding is vital if it is to be successful, because the colouring agent will only be taken up into the feathers when these are growing. It means that the colour food must be provided just prior to and throughout the moult, in order to obtain even plumage coloration which is vital for exhibition purposes. If the colouring process starts too late, then the first feathers to be replaced will be a lighter colour than the others, and a mottled effect will be the finished result.

It may be both easier and more beneficial to use a colouring softfood rather than a liquid, firstly because it avoids the need to mix the preparation with the bird's drinking water. It is harder to predict how much birds will drink, because this depends on their environment and their diet. They will obviously drink correspondingly more when the weather is warm for example, but less when they are being given fruit and greenstuff, as these contain relatively high percentages of water. The amount of the colouring agent consumed will vary from day to day on this basis.

Using a softfood is therefore a more reliable means of colour feeding, and it also boosts the protein intake of the birds' diet, at a time when the demands for protein are increased, as their new plumage grows. The softfood needs to be fed in basically the same way as eggfood. Virtually all brands available in this form can be offered straight from the packet, rather than having to be mixed with water, but always check the instructions in advance.

This also applies when using a liquid colour food. Although overdosing with a product of this type is not likely to be deadly, it will result

◆ LEFT

Intensive red-brown coloured canary. Colour food improves the coloration of such canaries, providing more contrast in the plumage, as well as emphasizing their reddish coloration.

they shouldn't be; this has as much to do with the amount of time and money the owner is prepared to spend managing their bird's feeding plan as anything else.

Among foreign birds, the familiar pink coloration of captive flamingos is maintained by well-managed colour feeding, while among aviary species, male weavers such as the orange bishop may benefit from being colour fed, as may sunbirds, which have areas of bright red plumage. Much will depend on the birds' normal diet however, with any fall-off in the depth of feather coloration occurring progressively over several moults, rather than suddenly over just a few weeks.

Although cayenne pepper is no longer used as a natural colouring agent, the addition of fresh carrots in some form to the diet of foreign birds will help to maintain their coloration, without the use of commercial synthetic preparations. Carrots contain a carotenoid colouring agent which is incorporated into the feathers. Small amounts of carrot juice given to the birds can have the same effect as a serving of grated or diced carrot.

YOUNG CANARIES

When canaries of those breeds which are colour-fed leave the nest, their plumage will be noticeably paler than that of adult birds. They can take their first colour feeds at the time when

they begin their first moult. The colour food at this early stage of the bird's life will deepen the feathering of the body plumage only, rather than that of the flight or tail feathers. This provides a means of aging young canaries, as it is not until the bird's first full moult that the bigger flight and tail feathers are replaced. Until this stage, the young canaries are described as unflighted, or sometimes as non-flighted, and they must be exhibited accordingly in the appropriate classes at bird shows. Once the early feathers have been shed, the birds can be described as flighted, which indicates that they are in full possession of coloured flight and tail feathers.

in the birds' droppings turning red in the short-term, and will cause emerging feathers to have an unwanted burnished appearance. There is nothing that can be done under these circumstances, and unfortunately, this means that the bird's exhibition potential will be spoilt until these feathers are shed again at the next moult.

COLOUR-FED BIRDS

Colour feeding is most commonly practised in a number of the canary breeds being kept for exhibition purposes – notably the Norwich, Yorkshire fancy, and lizard canaries, as well as new colour variants, such as the red factor. Mules, too, may be colour-fed, in order to emphasise the existing red coloration in their plumage. Birds that are kept as companions, rather than as exhibition stock, are not often colour fed, although there is no real reason why

◆ LEFT

Colour feeding can be very important for exhibition birds, helping to ensure that they catch the judge's eye, but it is not permitted under the show rules in every case.

CARING FOR
A PET BIRD

Looking after a pet bird is not difficult, but it helps to develop a set routine, which your bird will come to recognize. If you uncover its quarters in the morning and greet it with the words "good morning", you will find that the bird soon responds to you in a similar fashion.

Pet birds generally need to be fed once a day, preferably first thing in the morning, particularly if you are supplying fresh food of any kind. Birds are less likely to eat fruit or vegetables when they are just going to roost, so fresh food offered then will effectively be wasted. It will have to be removed in the morning if the leaves have wilted and before it can turn mouldy.

◆ OPPOSITE
Parrots will become bored if left on their own for long periods, so it may be better to start out with two at the outset, to keep each other company. A pair of Goffin's cockatoos is shown here.

◆ LEFT
Smaller parrots, such as this peach-faced lovebird, are often easier to manage in the home than in an aviary. This particular African species is now being bred in a wide range of colours.

POSITIONING THE CAGE

The location of the bird's quarters in the room is important, especially for a new arrival, to give it a sense of security and to help it settle in its new surroundings. It helps if the cage is kept at eye level, preferably in the corner of the room or along a wall, rather than in the centre. Never place the bird directly in front of the window. Not only may this attract potential bird thieves, but it could prove fatal for your pet in hot weather. The bird could succumb to heat stroke, unable to escape from the sun. Although many parrots do come from the warmer parts of the world, they rest in the trees, seeking cover during the day when the sun is at its hottest.

You may have a suitable piece of furniture on which to put the cage; alternatively, you could invest in a special cage stand. Be sure that this is secure, particularly if you have young children who may try to reach the bird by attempting to climb up the stand, pulling it over with potentially dire consequences for all involved. Larger flight cages, even those that do not extend down to the ground, are usually equipped with castors, which means they are free-standing, and can be moved around when necessary.

Covering the cage is a good idea if you stay up late in the evenings. It is not recommended to expose birds to more than 12 hours of light each day because this may affect their moulting cycle, causing them to suffer what is sometimes described as a "soft moult" – they drop feathers all the time rather than having distinct moulting periods like birds in outdoor aviaries. Covers designed for the purpose may be hard to find, but you can use a sheet or blanket; never use a woollen cover, as the bird may become caught up by its claws, and be injured.

Parrot cages for the home usually comprise of a wire top mounted on a solid base. These birds enjoy climbing around their quarters, so it is a good idea to place a screen behind the cage if it is located close to a wall, in order to protect the wallpaper from bird droppings and scattered pieces of fruit, which might otherwise stick there.

◆ LEFT
It is a good idea to cover your bird's cage if you stay up late, because even in the tropics, birds are exposed to a maximum of 12 hours of daylight, and a longer period could trigger persistent moulting.

MAKING THE ROOM SAFE

◆ BELOW

Be sure the room is safe, with all doors and windows closed, and other pets, such as cats, excluded before you allow your bird out of its quarters. Establish a routine to prevent mishaps.

◆ BELOW

The length of time a bird spends out in the room depends on you. Never be tempted to leave a bird out on its own. There could be other less obvious dangers, such as flaking paintwork.

It is very important to allow your bird out of its quarters regularly, to prevent it from becoming bored and to allow it to exercise. Birds generally follow a routine once they are used to being out of their quarters, and there are toys that you can offer so that it does not wreak havoc in the room.

You will need to prepare the room with your bird's safety in mind. First and foremost, ensure curtains can be drawn over the windows to prevent the bird from attempting to fly through the glass; otherwise a fatal brain haemorrhage or a broken neck could be the result.

Other pets, especially cats, must be excluded from the room, and the door kept closed. If you have a fire of any kind, this must be properly shielded with a guard, so that there is no risk of the bird burning itself. Electrical cables can be equally hazardous, particularly if you have a large parrot – its bill will be strong enough to cut through the flex. Check that electrical appliances not in use are switched off, and their plugs are disconnected.

Remove any potentially dangerous plants, such as cacti with sharp spines, as well as those which are likely to be poisonous. It is also a good idea to move valuable or treasured ornaments, just in case they are knocked over when the bird flies around the room.

Accidents of this type are most likely to occur when the bird is not used to being at liberty in the room, and so flies around without having anywhere to land comfortably. It may flop down clumsily as a result. For budgerigars, provide perches in prominent locations, where the bird can rest easily. For larger parrots, there are perch systems, which are intended to rest on top of cages, as well as free-standing exercise gyms. Once the novelty of coming out of its quarters subsides, a parrot will soon be content to spend much of its time playing and resting on equipment of this type.

When you let your bird out for the first time, allow it to come out on its own, rather than removing it from its quarters – there is more chance of it returning of its own accord. At first, though, be prepared to catch it to put it back in; for this it will help if the bird is hand-tame. Follow the same routine each day; the bird will soon get to know when it is time to return to its quarters and is likely to do so of its own accord. If you find that your bird is flying around wildly and is difficult to catch, draw the curtains, equip yourself with a torch and wait for the bird to settle in a convenient place. Switch out the light and, using the torch, move cautiously towards the bird. You should be able to catch it easily in the dark.

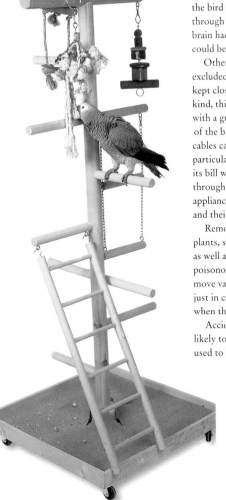

◆ LEFT

A typical playstand for a parrot, mounted on castors so that it can be wheeled from room to room. An array of toys will keep the bird occupied.

KEEPING CLEAN

♦ BELOW
In the case of a pet budgerigar, special sandsheets are available in a range of sizes to line the floor of the cage. This covering will need to be changed at least twice a week.

How often you clean the cage depends to some extent on the type of bird you are keeping. Mynahs in particular are very messy and must be cleaned out every day. For parrots, on the other hand, cleaning every two or three days is adequate, with a weekly scrubbing of their food and water containers. Cages which have a coating on their bars are easy to wipe clean, if some fruit becomes smeared on them for example, although it is still a good idea to dismantle the cage and wash it thoroughly every few months. Special disinfectants are available for use on avian equipment; these are quite safe if the instructions are followed. In some designs of budgerigar cage, the top and base units may separate for cleaning purposes. Always double check when reassembling them that they are properly joined together. Otherwise, if you pick the cage up by the hook on its roof, the bottom may fall away, allowing the bird to escape into the room.

Perches must be kept clean, and will need replacing from time to time – frequently in the case of parrots, which will whittle them away with their powerful bills.

CAGE FLOOR COVERINGS

Sandsheets are traditional for use with budgerigars and canaries. Different sizes are available so that it is not necessary to overlap the sheets, which are relatively expensive. By way of economy, some owners tip the seed husks into a rubbish bag and scrape off the droppings, two or three times, replacing the sandsheet once a week. Hen budgerigars usually start to shred their sandsheets when they approach breeding condition. This is normal

behaviour and no cause for concern.

Another option, less expensive than sandsheets, is loose bird sand, which is often blended with a little oyster shell grit. As the bird flies, its wing movements may disturb the sand, so a suitably thick layer is required in order to prevent some areas of the tray from being left uncovered, which will ultimately make it harder to clean. There are some other drawbacks to using sand, not least of which is that it is heavy to carry, which in turn may make it difficult to dispose of, particularly if you live in an apartment. Also, it can be scattered outside the confines of the bird's quarters quite easily, and it is not advisable to use it if a hen bird shows signs of becoming broody. When spending time on the floor of its cage, some of the sand may

work its way into the bird's vent, causing serious irritation.

A major drawback of using bird sand in cages housing mynahs or parrots is that any fruit which falls on to the floor will be contaminated with particles of sand. This is why it is important to use only specially prepared bird sand, rather than cheaper alternatives available from builders' outlets, which may not be clean. It may be better to use one of the other commercially available floor coverings for parrots, provided absorbency is good. The floor covering for mynah birds should be absorbent. A thick layer of newspaper can be used for them because, unlike parrots, mynahs are unlikely to shred the paper. Mynah birds will need their floor covering changed every day.

◆ BELOW
A stainless steel pot, suitable for feeding smaller
birds such as finches. Although easy to clean,
it is relatively light and could be tipped over
easily by bigger birds perching on the rim.

◆ BELOW
Feeding pots are available in a variety of sizes,
with plastic containers on the left and a ceramic
bowl on the right. These should always be
positioned so they are not beneath perches.

CONTAINER CARE

Food and water pots should be cleaned
every day. The food pots should be
washed out with a detergent, rinsed
thoroughly and dried with a paper
towel, before being refilled. This will
ensure that there is no stale food
which could harm your bird's health,
nor will its quarters start to develop
an unpleasant odour.

Unlike parrots, mynah birds
need to be provided with an
open water pot, rather than
a drinking bottle, because of
their pointed bills. Wash this
container like the food pot:
wipe with a paper towel to
ensure the interior is clean, before
rinsing and refilling it. Most mynah
cages are of a box-type design, open
just at the front to prevent droppings

being scattered around the room.
Cages of this type are usually
equipped with pots that fit securely in
place in the cage front so they cannot
be dislodged.

These members of the starling
family are very keen bathers, and
should be provided with a clean bowl
of water for this purpose. In the
absence of one of these, they are likely
to resort to bathing in their water pot,
which can become contaminated as a
result. Choose a heavy earthenware
container of the type sold for dogs, so
that there is no risk of the bowl being
tipped over, spilling the water all over
the floor of the cage.

◆ BELOW
Offering food from your hand
can build a strong bond between
pet and owner, as shown in
the case of this young cock
budgerigar. Note that if your
pet bird's appetite unexpectedly
declines, this could be a sign of
impending illness.

TAMING A PET BIRD

If you start out with a young budgerigar or hand-reared parrot, the likelihood is that it will already be hand-tame. Any bird will need a few days to adjust to its new surroundings, and it may take even longer for it to become used to you, especially in the case of a parrot that has been reared from the egg by one person.

Although individual birds differ in their training responses, you will inevitably need to be patient with your new pet. Regular short training sessions, three or four times every day, are likely to be far more useful than the occasional marathon, especially as birds have a relatively short attention span and are likely to be bored by the proceedings after five minutes or so. You may be able to speed up winning your pet's confidence by offering a piece of fruit, for example, in your other hand. This means that not only will the bird have to step on to your hand in order to reach the tidbit, it will have to stay there to eat it.

Start the taming regime by offering tidbits and encouraging the bird to step on to your hand. Place your hand parallel with the perch, and gently lift the bird's toes up, so that it transfers its grip forward to your hand. Keep your hand level, so that the parrot has no difficulty in keeping its grip. For a budgerigar, use the index finger of one hand rather than your whole hand, to ensure that the bird can maintain a firm grip – otherwise, it will step off your hand. For larger parrots, bear in mind that, particularly as youngsters, their claws tend to be much sharper than those of adult birds, and so it is a good idea to wear a pair of thin leather gloves during the training process, to avoid painful scratches. In due course, after several weeks of perching properly, the sharp tips will be worn down. If you are scratched, wash the wound thoroughly and apply an antiseptic cream.

Once the bird is sufficiently confident to step on to your hand, the next stage is to take it out of its quarters in the same way. At first, you may find that it hops off at the last minute, particularly if the door opening is not very large. Try to persuade it to step across from one hand to the other, positioned just outside the cage. Before long the bird will realize that it can step out through the opening, or it may clamber round on the mesh. If possible, avoid the situation where you have to restrain the bird in order to take it out through the door. Most birds resent being held, and this will interfere with the training process. On release, your pet is likely to try to fly off, rather than continuing to perch on your hand.

In the room, it is useful to perch-train your pet. This entails using a relatively short length of perch, placed up near the bird, on to which it will step readily, should it be out of reach of your hand. You can carry the bird back to its quarters on this perch, if it can't be tempted on to your hand.

In many cases, parrots like to rest on their owner's shoulder, but be certain to remove any earrings beforehand or your parrot may try to remove them itself. It might even nibble at your ear, with painful consequences. It may be worthwhile investing in, or even making, a protective pad to fit over your

HAND-TAMING A PARROT

1 Once you have encouraged a bird out of its quarters, the next stage is to persuade it on to your hand. A bird will respond more readily if a piece of fruit is offered as a reward.

2 Keep your hand at perch level and place a finger in front of the bird's toes. Hold out the tidbit to tempt the bird on to your hand. Wear protective gloves if the bird's claws are very sharp.

3 Feed the bird the tidbit treat when it has stepped on to your hand, in order to build his trust in you. If the bird is a new recruit, end the training session now, before it becomes bored.

shoulder, so there will be no risk of the bird damaging your clothing directly with its claws, or soiling it when perching there.

TEACHING A BIRD TO TALK

You can start teaching your bird to talk almost as soon as you acquire it. Some young hand-reared parrots may already be starting to speak, although there are individual differences. Young grey parrots have the potential to develop into the most effective mimics – both speaking with clarity and also whistling tunes – but according to studies in this field, they may make no attempt to mimic human speech until they are at least six months old.

As well as its own abilities, the bird's teacher has a direct effect on its talking skill. Birds generally find it easier to pick up words from women or children because of their higher pitch. Again, several short sessions through the day are likely to give the best results, with no distractions in the form of other people or noise. You should have your bird's entire concentration. Repeat the chosen word or phrase slowly and clearly, giving the bird an opportunity to respond before progressing.

You may find that the first words are uttered when you are out of the room, almost as if the bird is practising its speech by itself. Do not rush the bird by trying to expand its vocabulary rapidly; this will only confuse it. Instead, gradually add new words while not neglecting the old ones, which may otherwise be forgotten. An essential piece of information to teach your bird at an early stage is your telephone number; then if it does escape, whoever finds it will be able to contact you.

Mynah birds are excellent mimics, and can learn to repeat the ring of the telephone and the doorbell with unerring accuracy. Keep these birds out of earshot of these sounds, if possible, to ensure you are able to distinguish between them.

BATHING

Birds housed indoors must have the opportunity to bathe regularly, in order to keep their plumage in good condition. This is naturally achieved by means of a waterproofing oil released from the preen gland, a slightly swollen area, which is normally hidden under the feathering at the base of the tail. The readiness of birds to bathe in a pot of water differs according to the species and the individual. Mynahs will do so readily almost every day. While some budgerigars will regularly use a plastic bath attached around the entrance to their cage, others may be more reluctant to do so, in which case they will need to be sprayed twice a week.

Buy a plant sprayer, clean it out, fill with tepid water and set the nozzle to spray a fine mist. Remove food containers from the bird's quarters before spraying. The best time to do it is just before cleaning out the cage because the water will also help to damp down feather dust lying on the tray. Do not point the nozzle directly at the bird; aim slightly above its head, so that the droplets fall down like rain. On the first few occasions, the bird may be nervous, squawking and moving around its quarters, but this will soon pass and before long it will be waiting to be sprayed. This will be followed by an intense session of preening, after which the feathers will look immaculate. Regular spraying should help to prevent a parrot from plucking its feathers, which can be a particular problem in the case of household pet birds.

♦ LEFT
Some parrots make better talkers than others but much will also depend on the teaching plan; hand-reared parrots are often encouraged from an early age to mimic speech.

CARING FOR AVIARY BIRDS

In the aviary, new birds are likely to be nervous for the first few weeks, until they have settled down. This applies especially to Australian parakeets, as well as pigeons and doves, which will fly around wildly at first if disturbed unexpectedly. It is therefore a good idea to be sure everything is in place, even the water drinkers, before releasing the birds into their new home.

Confine them to the aviary shelter at first, where they will find their food and water without difficulty and have time to settle. If they have access to the flight, they may fly straight out and stay there, resolutely refusing to return under cover. You will have no option but to catch them up and return them to the shelter, which will be upsetting for them.

When the time comes to allow the birds out into the flight, choose a day when the weather is likely to be fine and settled for a period. If the birds, especially softbills, are out in a downpour, they may become waterlogged and unable to fly. They will have to be allowed to dry off indoors, before being returned to the aviary. This is one reason why it is important to spray birds that are being temporarily housed indoors, so that the natural waterproofing on their plumage is not lost.

◆ OPPOSITE
Cleanliness is especially important in a colony aviary, such as this, where a number of birds are housed. Establish a regular cleaning routine and keep to it.

◆ LEFT
When catching a bird for any reason, close your hand lightly around its body, so as not to cause undue distress, or any damage to its plumage.

EVERYDAY CARE

◆ LEFT
If your bird's behaviour changes suddenly, and
it will not fly normally, a close inspection of the
wings may reveal the reason why.

Everyone develops their own system for looking after their own birds, but it is important that you find time each day to look at them carefully. This is the best way to recognize when a bird is off-colour, before any more obvious signs of illness develop.

Birds are very adept at masking signs of injury until they are seriously ill. A bird is usually less active in the early stages of ill-health, perhaps flying from a perch momentarily later than a group of others. If you notice an individual bird looking at you from one angle, for example, this may be an indication that its other eye is infected or swollen, impairing its vision. Something like this is easy to miss if you are hurrying to feed and water your stock in the morning before heading off to work.

The risk of illness arising is most likely in the first few months of setting up the aviary, when the birds are adjusting to their surroundings and often to different food as well. Once new birds are settled, and providing they are housed in clean surroundings and are well-fed, you are unlikely to encounter significant health problems. This is especially true if the birds are housed in pairs rather than in a colony.

FEEDING CONTAINERS

Always provide food and water in the aviary shelter rather than in the flight – seed in particular is less likely to attract the attention of rodents, and the food will remain dry, which is important because damp seed can rapidly turn mouldy. Mould represents a serious threat to birds' health.

If you have a hopper for budgerigars, this will keep their seed free from any droppings, with the husks falling down into the tray beneath, which helps to keep the floor clean. For other birds, different types of feeding containers are necessary. Hook-on plastic food containers can be used for various species, including finches and softbills, but they are less suitable for parrots because parrots may dislodge them, scattering the contents on the floor. The plastic is also unlikely to be robust enough to

◆ LEFT
These metal containers are sufficiently robust for use with large parrots, which are likely to destroy plastic pots of a similar size.

◆ FAR LEFT
Some birds, such as quails, feed on the floor, and will often eat seed spilt by birds perching above them. Even so, they should always be provided with their own supplies of food and water.

◆ LEFT
Flowers have been provided to supply nectar and pollen to these Goldie's lorikeets.

CARING FOR NECTAR FEEDERS

Hygiene is especially important for nectar feeders. Their drinkers must be washed out at least once a day. It helps to have two sets, so that one can be left soaking in a disinfectant solution while the other is in use. Use a jug to measure out the correct volume of nectar, and stir this in water thoroughly so that it dissolves completely. Do not mix more than you need for a single feed; discard any excess. During hot weather, you may have to prepare two feeds a day.

withstand the bills of the larger species. With containers of this type, it is important to position them near a perch, so the birds have easy access.

It may be possible to attach food containers to the mesh used for covering the window. For softbills, the mesh must be on a removable framework so you can wash the window behind, which will inevitably become soiled with scattered food. Another alternative is to knock two netting staples into the wood of the shelter itself, through which you can drop the supports for the container. Make sure that these are held firmly in place because if the container tilts forwards, there will be more wastage.

For parrots, choose heavy-duty metal, hook-on containers, attaching them to the side of the aviary. Some designs come equipped with a pot that screws on to a supporting bracket, enabling them to be placed close to a perch. Alternatively, heavy-duty earthenware pots can be used, although they will have to be supported on a feeding tray, rather like a bird table. The top must be easy to wipe clean, with no nooks or crannies.

This option is also a possibility for softbills, but bear in mind that a single feeding station may be inadequate, especially at the approach of the breeding season. The cock bird may be chasing the hen to the extent that she

cannot eat at the main feeding site without being persecuted, so that a second site will be required. Occasionally, this occurs with parrots too, particularly the Eclectus (*Eclectus roratus*). These hens can prove to be very assertive over cock birds.

Food must be provided on the aviary's floor for those species that are primarily ground-dwelling, including pheasants and quails. Quails can be very wasteful in their feeding habits, scattering seed widely, so a special feeder is needed to counteract this. Hopper-type feeders can be used for pheasants, but make sure that the flow of food does not become obstructed at any stage.

✦ TOP
Hummingbirds are unique in that they can hover in front of their food source. For other nectivores, place the nectar supply next to a perch for easy access.

✦ LEFT
Always ensure that the aviary floor area is kept clean, particularly where food supplies are located. Otherwise, birds may pick up enteric infections.

◆ LEFT AND BELOW
Ensuring birds have an
uncontaminated supply of fresh
drinking water is very important.
Use a water fountain for this purpose.

◆ LEFT AND BELOW
Drinkers should always be
positioned out of direct sunlight.
Otherwise, they will be prone to
a rapid spread of algal growth.

WATER CONTAINERS

Drinkers should be located inside the
shelter, partly because they are less
likely to freeze during spells of cold
weather. Tubular drinkers can be used
for finches, budgerigars and birds of
similar size. These are supplied with
special clips to hold them in place on
the mesh. There are also bottle
drinkers, intended for parrots, that
have a ball reservoir to stop the flow
when the drinker is not in use. These
drinkers must not be filled to
maximum capacity in cold weather,

because as water freezes it expands,
and the drinker may split. Allow the
drinkers to thaw out gently in a clean
bucket of warm water. When refilling
the bottle types, ensure that the water
can flow freely through the spout –
often there is a hidden plug of ice
between the two ball valves. You can
check this quite easily by holding up
the nozzle and seeing if the ball in
the spout slips back into the spout.

Although these drinkers provide
clean water, they are easily detached
from the mesh by a mischievous

◆ ABOVE LEFT
Birds must always have easy access to fresh
drinking water. A typical drinker, which is ideal
for breeding cages, attached to the outside of
the cage.

◆ FAR LEFT
This type of drinker needs to be securely
suspended by the metal loop from the mesh
or a perch in the aviary.

◆ LEFT
A plastic water fountain can be placed on the
aviary floor, and is recommended for quails,
which spend their time at ground level. It can
also be used for pigeons and doves.

1 Birds in a birdroom are not affected by the noise of a vacuum cleaner. This type of equipment is very useful at preventing the build-up of dust in the bird's environment.

2 One of the advantages of having a solid floor in the birdroom is that it can be cleaned and disinfected easily. This is especially important in this part of the aviary, where the birds are fed.

parrot; some parrots can even manage to puncture the plastic of the bottle. It is advisable, therefore, to invest in a protective guard so the birds are not left without water at any stage. This can be critical, particularly if there are young chicks in the nest, because they are susceptible to dehydration.

Large plastic drinkers are suitable for pheasants and quails; place these on the floor of the shelter, taking care that they are not overhung by perches, or the water could be soiled from above. The birds should be provided with fresh water every day. Bacteria that pose a serious threat to the birds' health can multiply rapidly in stale or dirty water.

When it comes to washing out water containers, these should be scrubbed out with a bottle brush of the appropriate size, partly to prevent the development of green algal growth up the sides. It is especially important to wash out the drinkers if a food supplement has been added to the drinking water. Use a detergent and disinfectant before rinsing out the container thoroughly and refilling it with fresh water.

AVIARY MAINTENANCE

Once the aviary is occupied, the shelter will need to be cleaned every week. If you use newspaper on the floor, simply fold up the old sheets and discard them. Replace them with fresh sheets and, if necessary, stick down the overlying sections using adhesive tape, so that they will not be disturbed by the birds flying around.

Around the perimeter of the aviary, keep the grass cut reasonably short. Long grass provides vital camouflage for rodents, especially rats. Rats represent a real hazard, because not only can they spread serious diseases such as pseudotuberculosis, but they may also harm the birds directly, particularly if they are breeding. Sound footings and underlying the floor of the entire aviary with mesh are the best defences. Any tunnelling activity in the floor is indicative of rats, although you are unlikely to see them. The safest option is to transfer the birds elsewhere while you deal with the rodents, but if this is not feasible, invest in a live trap, which should be set overnight after an initial period of simply being baited. Once

you are sure that the rat or rats are entering it, the trap can be primed. Break-back traps should never be used in the presence of birds, nor should any poisons.

It is vital to act as soon as you see any signs of rodents, because otherwise you could soon be overrun with them, such is their reproductive potential. While rats tend to burrow in, mice will slip in through any gaps, sometimes even squeezing beneath an ill-fitting door. Mice may start breeding in aviary surroundings almost immediately after gaining access, often invading the space behind the shelter lining. Hardboard is no match for their sharp teeth. The only solution is to remove the lining and flush out the rodents directly. You will know if mice are present by their droppings in the vicinity of the food pots and the strong odour of their urine, which pervades a closed space. A live trap will catch a number at a single setting, without any risk to the birds, which will not need to be removed. These traps are highly effective in most cases, and unlike rats, mice do not appear to become suspicious of traps.

CATCHING AND HANDLING AVIARY BIRDS

It is inevitable that at some point you will have to catch birds in the aviary. This can be stressful, for both you and the birds, and must be carried out with care to prevent injuries.

Do not try to catch any birds when the weather is hot, but wait until the relative cool of the morning. Take down perches that will restrict your ability to move around the aviary. It is easier to catch a bird in the shelter, so go into the flight and encourage the birds to fly back into the shelter; you can confine them there by closing the birds' entry hatch. Some birds are easier to catch than others because they are slower in flight. Some, such as parrots, can inflict a painful bite, so it is a good idea to wear protective gloves.

Bird nets are available in different sizes. If you decide to use a net, which can be helpful with smaller birds such as finches, it is important that the rim is well padded. Even so, this is no guarantee that you will not injure the bird as you catch it. The net should be a good depth, so that once a bird has

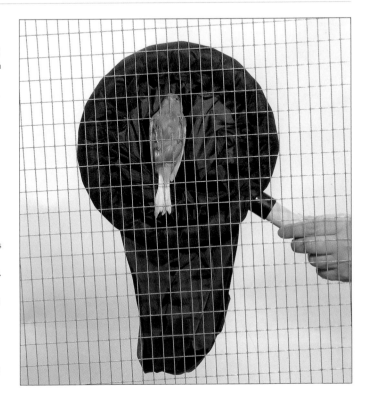

♦ BELOW
Lift a bird very carefully out of the net. Most birds anchor their claws into the material, and these will need to be freed first.

been caught, you can grip the material at the top, below the rim, to stop it flying out again. Use the net when a bird is on the ground or on the mesh; it is difficult to catch a bird in flight.

Have a ventilated wooden box with a secure lid within reach, so you can put the bird into it quickly. If put in a cage at this point, the bird is likely to fly around wildly and may damage its plumage or injure itself. You may not even have to pick the bird out of the net. Invert the net gently above the open carrying box. If you need to free the bird, use your left hand (assuming you are right-handed). With your right hand, hold the rim of the net, tilting it

◆ BELOW
Pheasants can be restrained by carefully holding them at the top of their legs, but you must take care to ensure they do not struggle and injure themselves as a result.

◆ RIGHT
Parrots can inflict a painful bite, and although young birds may be handled with the help of a towel, as here, older individuals will be more safely restrained if you are wearing gloves.

over to prevent the bird from flying out. Place your left hand inside and feel your way down to the bird's head. Put your first and second fingers gently around the sides of its neck, and wrap your other fingers around its body. With its wings now secured in your palm, the bird will cease to struggle and you can lift it out. This movement will cause the bird to tighten its grip on the net, using its claws, so once the bird is restrained, lay the net on the ground and use your hand to prise the claws free.

Always aim to catch even smaller birds individually, rather than two or three together. This will make it easier, and will reduce the risk of injury.

LOST BIRDS

Escapes can happen at any time, but if you have a safety porch attached to your aviary, the likelihood of any birds slipping past you and out of the aviary is very remote. If a bird does fly into the safety porch as you enter the aviary, it can be encouraged to fly back into the aviary without difficulty. Problems are more likely to arise as the result of damage to the aviary. Storms and high winds are a particular problem, so if you live in an area prone to severe weather, it is important to ensure the aviary is carefully sited and solidly anchored to its foundations. Vandals too can cause the escape of birds, which is why the external

door to an aviary should always be padlocked, as a basic security measure.

If you do lose a bird, the first thing will be to keep watch in the vicinity of the aviary to see if it returns of its own accord. This is very likely with species which possess good homing instincts, such as doves; other species – parakeets, for example – will often fly off wildly, and may end up some distance away from home.

Unless the bird is exhausted, trying to catch it with a net will require considerable guile: move very slowly so as not to frighten it. If there is no sighting of your escapee, contact neighbours, local bird clubs and animal welfare organizations, in case someone has seen or already caught your bird.

The length of time that an escapee can survive depends on the species and the individual bird. It also depends on the time of year, since in late summer, food will be more readily available and the weather will be warmer than in the wintertime.

BUYING BIRDS

The choice of where to buy a bird will depend on the species you are seeking and where you live. It is preferable to find a local source of supply, but in some cases, you may have to travel some distance. Bird-keeping publications are a useful source of information. If you are interested in establishing an exhibition stud, it is worth reading the show reports regularly, and attending as many shows as possible, to familiarize yourself with the type of birds that are catching the judges' eyes, and the breeders who are winning consistently.

In other cases, with parrots for example, you may be able to find a breeder via one of the many parrot-keeping organizations which now exist. Again, look in the bird-keeping press or try a search on the Internet, as many specialist organizations now have their own websites. Many such clubs organize sales days, where a number of different bird species will be available to buy. In comparison, most pet stores only stock a limited range of birds. They may be able to source a particular bird for you, but if there is a bird farm in your area, you will not only find a wider range of birds on offer, but you will also be able to pick up expert tips on their care.

♦ OPPOSITE
If a bird catches your eye on a visit to a
bird garden or zoo, take the opportunity to
find out the name of the species as a way of
increasing your knowledge of bird breeds.

♦ LEFT
It can be impossible to age birds reliably
once they have moulted into adult
plumage, unless they are rung with a band
confirming the year when they hatched.

MAKING YOUR CHOICE

Never rush into a decision – if you feel
unhappy for any reason, it is better
not to buy the bird. If you are seeking
a hand-reared parrot, you may need
to be patient. There is usually a good
supply of hand-reared grey parrots
available throughout the year, but the
breeding season of other species, such
as Amazons, tends to be much more
restricted. As a consequence, young
Amazon parrots are likely to be on
offer in the greatest numbers at one
time of the year only, the early autumn
in northern temperate latitudes.

Should you be looking for aviary
stock, bear in mind that if you
purchase birds from the late summer
onwards, there will be no possibility
of them becoming acclimatized before
the onset of winter if they have not
been outside or have been recently

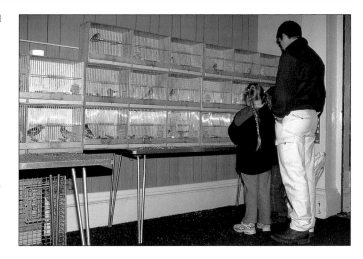

♦ ABOVE
Sale days organized by bird societies are a good
way of obtaining new stock, and will provide an
opportunity to discuss bird care with breeders.

♦ BELOW
Do not feel rushed into making a purchase. You
must allow time to look at the birds properly, to
ensure as far as possible that they are healthy.

♦ BELOW
Special travelling boxes are available for birds.
Cardboard boxes, such as this, are suitable for
smaller birds, but use the more robust plywood
structures for strong-billed parrots.

♦ LEFT
Take the opportunity
to ask the breeder
any questions you
may have regarding
both the life history
of the bird, and the
type of food they
have been receiving.

imported, and so you must be
prepared to keep them indoors until
the spring.

The price of birds can vary
dramatically, even in the case of the
same species. Expect to pay more for
established stock, and also for true
pairs, rather than unsexed individuals,
in the case of those species where it is
not possible to distinguish between
the sexes visually. A premium price is
usually attached to proven pairs of
the larger parrots; here, compatibility
between members of a pair is an
important aspect in terms of achieving
breeding success. Simply having two
birds of the opposite gender is no
guarantee that they will form a pair,
bond, and mate successfully, no
matter how long you wait for them.

♦ BELOW
Find out if the birds have been kept indoors.
It is inadvisable to allow them into an outdoor
aviary until all risk of frost has passed.

With birds where compatibility is
not a problem, such as budgerigars,
pricing may be influenced by the bird's
coloration. Blue series individuals, such
as cobalts and violets, as well as bright
coloured lutinos, sell for more than
a green or grey bird. With exhibition
stock, however, the price depends not
on the bird's colour, but on its pedigree
and the success-rate of the breeder
concerned. Birds from a breeder who
wins consistently at high levels will
cost more than birds from a novice.

WHAT TO LOOK FOR

When faced with an aviary full of birds for sale, it is a considerable help to have a clear idea of what you are looking for. As a general indication, the bird should be lively and flying readily, and its plumage should look in good condition, although in the case of a young hand-reared chick, its feathers may not be as sleek as those of an older bird. Do not be tempted to buy a chick before it is capable of feeding on its own; the weaning phase can be traumatic, and the risk of problems arising is increased if the chick has recently been rehomed.

♦ ABOVE
A mature cock budgerigar. It is usually possible to distinguish between young fledglings and adult birds, but it is not easy to age adult birds, unless they have been banded with a closed ring.

Check the bird's eyes, which should be bright, with no signs of swelling. Diamond doves are the notable exception here; swelling of the peri-orbital skin around the eyes is associated with cock birds of the species when in breeding condition.

Check the feet for signs of swelling or difficulty in perching. If you plan to exhibit your bird, it is vital to ensure that it possesses a full complement of claws. Look at the balls of the feet for any obvious inflammation.

♦ LEFT
There is usually nothing seriously wrong if a bird is feeding properly, but a closer check will still be needed.

♦ BELOW LEFT
It is possible to age African grey parrots by the coloration of their irises. In young birds, these are dark.

♦ BELOW RIGHT
This is the typical yellow iris coloration of an adult African grey. Adult birds do not make good pets, unless they are tame and talking, but they should settle well in aviary surroundings.

A closer examination will be needed once the bird has been caught. Look carefully to ensure the nostrils are of even size, and are not blocked. Any enlargement of the nostrils may be indicative of a long-standing infection that could flare up again. This is often a problem with grey parrots.

The bill itself should be free from any damage, and not overgrown. Budgerigars sometimes suffer from undershot bills, where the upper part of the bill does not curve down over

◆ BELOW
Heavily scaled legs, especially in the case of
finches, canaries and softbills, are often a sign
of old age. They may also be indicative of the
parasitic illness known as scaly leg.

◆ BELOW
Always check the claws, particularly if you are
hoping to show the bird. Damaged or missing
claws will ruin any competition chances,
although overgrown claws are easily remedied.

the lower part, but curls back within
it. This problem can often be traced
back to poor nest hygiene, resulting
in nest dirt hardening and distorting
the growth of the bill, although it may
also be an inherited condition. In
either instance, there is nothing that
can be done to correct the deformity,
other than trimming back the lower
bill. Without the constraint of an
overlapping upper bill, this will grow
more readily than is usual and will
have to be trimmed back regularly for
the rest of the bird's life.

Another problem that can affect
the bills of budgerigars is scaly face.
This is caused by a mite and will
spread readily if untreated, causing
permanent distortion of the bill. In
the initial stages, scaly face shows up
as tiny snail-like tracks running across
the upper bill. The more characteristic
coral-like encrustations develop later.

The overall condition of the bird is
most reliably assessed from examining
the breastbone, which lies in the
midline of the body, just below the
neck. This should be well covered with
muscle; distinct hollows either side are
a cause for concern, indicating that the
bird is underweight. This could mean
that it has not been eating properly, or

it could be suffering from intestinal
roundworms, or a more serious
chronic illness, such as an internal
tumour. Buying birds in such
condition is therefore a decided risk,
particularly if there is staining of the
feathering around the vent, which
indicates a digestive disturbance.

It is impossible to age birds reliably
once they have moulted into adult
plumage. In the case of finches and
softbills, the legs may provide a clue –
heavy scaling tends to indicate an
older individual, although it would be
more helpful to compare a group of
the same species.

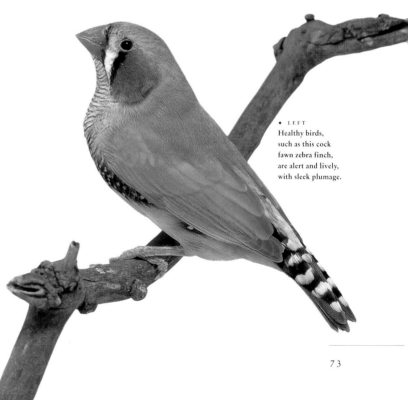

◆ LEFT
Healthy birds,
such as this cock
fawn zebra finch,
are alert and lively,
with sleek plumage.

◆ BELOW
A colony of peach-faced lovebirds. These
small parrots can be very aggressive and it is
important not to introduce a new individual
to an established group.

SETTLING IN A NEW ARRIVAL

Moving a bird to a new environment, particularly if there is a long journey involved, is likely to be stressful. Reducing the stress should mean that birds will settle down with minimal problems. Preparation is important. Have everything organized before the bird arrives so that you can simply transfer it to its new quarters.

Hand-reared birds are perhaps more vulnerable than most to digestive upsets, which means it is especially important to maintain them on their usual diet. Make any changes gradually after a couple of weeks or so. The same applies to softbills and all nectar-feeding birds because they are particularly prone to potentially fatal digestive upsets if their diet is suddenly changed.

You can minimize the likelihood of illness in the critical early days after acquiring a new bird by the use of an electrolyte and probiotic products. An electrolyte will help to restore the body's fluid balance, following a period when the bird may not have been eating and drinking normally. Probiotic food contains beneficial bacteria, like those in live yogurt, which will colonize the gut and stabilize its acidity, assisting the digestive process and making it much harder for potentially harmful microbes to gain access to the body via this route.

If you already have other birds, it is important to keep new arrivals away from them, to be sure that they do not

◆ LEFT
Australian parakeets
have a justifiable
reputation for being
very nervous when
first moved to new
surroundings. It may
be a good idea to let
them settle in an
aviary shelter at first.
Crimson rosellas,
also known as
Pennant's parakeets,
are shown here.

◆ BELOW
A parrot which has been in another home
will take time to adjust to new domestic
surroundings, particularly an older bird, such
as this grey. Breeding pairs may also be shy.

introduce any disease to your collection. Releasing a newly arrived bird straight into an existing collection also increases the stress on that bird because it may be bullied by the others. This, in turn, will increase the risk of it falling ill. Wait at least three weeks before adding a new bird to an existing collection, during which time you can have various tests carried out to establish the bird's state of health.

Faecal samples provide a simple means of determining whether the bird is suffering from intestinal roundworms, which can be a particular problem in Australian parakeets, while tapeworms may be present in ground-dwelling species which hunt invertebrates. The tests for these are not expensive and can save you introducing the parasites into the aviary, where they will be much harder, if not impossible, to eliminate. You would have to de-worm the birds regularly and often in order to ensure they remained healthy.

When you do decide to transfer new birds to existing accommodation,

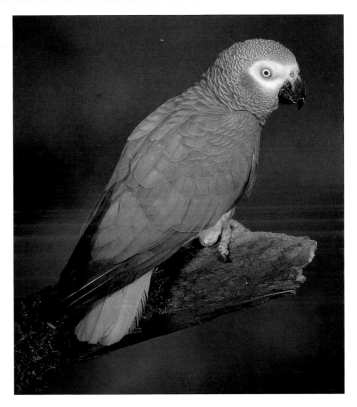

◆ BELOW
A parrot which has been in another home will take time to adjust to new domestic surroundings, particularly an older bird, such as this grey. Breeding pairs may also be shy.

◆ LEFT
Try to avoid introducing new birds to an aviary during the breeding season, because the likelihood of fighting breaking out is dramatically increased, as in the case of these two royal starlings.

moving them into an outside aviary for the first time, then it is a good idea to keep them confined in the shelter for the first few days. They will then return here to feed without fear in the future, and, hopefully, will roost here as well, particularly if the perches are positioned at a slightly higher level than in the flight.

When it comes to breeding, it can take some parrots several years to settle down to nesting, while Australian parakeets are likely to breed the following year. Certain birds may even nest soon after a move; this is most likely with domesticated finches.

ADDING TO AN EXISTING COLLECTION

Adding birds to an existing collection, rather than introducing a pair to an aviary on their own, can be a difficult process at any time of the year, and is especially problematic during the breeding season. It is usually better to wait until this period has passed, because otherwise the newcomer may be severely harassed – a hen in particular may be bullied by a would-be partner in its enthusiasm to breed. Australian parakeets, pheasants, quails, pigeons and doves rank among the worst offenders in this respect.

At other times, the intrusion of another bird or pair into an existing flock should be monitored carefully for signs of aggression from any of the established birds. It could be that introducing a bird of similar coloration, albeit of a different species, may lead to displays of aggression. Blue-capped waxbills (*Uraeginthus cyanocephala*), for example, will often react aggressively towards red-cheeked cordon bleus (*U. bengalus*) for this reason.

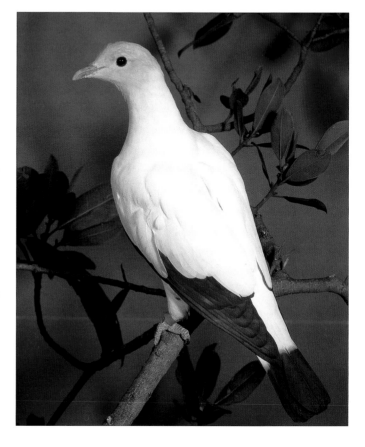

♦ ABOVE
Pigeons and doves, in spite of being seen as symbols of peace, are actually aggressive by nature, particularly when a new individual is added to an existing group.

♦ LEFT
The diamond dove is usually tolerant of the company of others of its kind. Compatibility is best achieved if the birds are all transferred to their aviary at the same time, prior to breeding.

conflict,
particularly
if the flight is
planted, with
plenty of retreats
available. Offer a
choice of feeding
locations to prevent the
cock bird monopolizing
one area and preventing
the hen from being able
to feed.

Within an established
colony, it is equally hazardous
to introduce a male newcomer
if the breeding season is underway.
You will need to wait until the end
of this period, when the birds are less
territorial and other changes are being
made to the flock. Again, when you
do introduce the newcomer, make sure
there is plenty of vegetation, and a
choice of feeding stations to ensure
that all birds have access to food.

AVOIDING CONFLICTS

In the case of birds which are likely
to be aggressive, it is better to remove
the established individual from the
aviary first for a few days, assuming
that alternative accommodation is
available. This is especially important
if you are intending to introduce a
hen to the aviary, as she is likely to
be harried relentlessly by the cock,
especially if acquired during the
breeding season.

Taking out the cock bird, and
replacing both cock and hen at the
same time, will reduce the risk of

Aggression is least likely to occur
with finches, and most common with
parrots, where the flock structure is
rigorously upheld against intruders.
Adding a different species, such as a
pair of diamond doves, to an aviary of
finches is unlikely to result in conflict.
Again, it is important not to do this
when the birds are nesting, because
the change in environment could cause
a nervous pair to abandon their nest.

The best time to add new bird stock
to the aviary is after the end of the
breeding period, when established
birds will be moulting. The greatest
selection of stock is available for sale
at this time, as breeders reduce their
bird collections at the end of the
breeding period.

Dealers, too, may have sales, but
beware of buying recently imported
birds at this time of year; it will be too
late to acclimatize them to an outside
aviary, and they will need to be housed
in heated winter-time quarters until
the following spring. If you intend to
overwinter your existing birds under
these conditions, you can introduce
the newcomers during this period, if
you are certain that they are healthy.
This will give the group time to settle
down before being released into their
breeding quarters in the spring.

◆ ABOVE
Red-cheeked cordon bleus do not agree well
with others of their own kind, but they are
generally compatible with other waxbills, and
with small, non-aggressive softbills and doves.

KEEPING BIRDS HEALTHY

Birds are most likely to fall ill soon after being moved to a new home, as they may encounter unfamiliar microbes or may not have been eating properly for several days. Once established in their quarters, however, and after moulting there for the first time, the risk of illness is greatly reduced.

Illness may also arise in a collection where a number of birds are being kept in the same aviary, budgerigars for example, rather than being housed on their own or in a pair, as in the case of a pair of parakeets.

Good hygiene plays a vital role in preventing the spread of infection in an aviary where a number of birds are present. This is not just a matter of keeping the aviary floor clean, but also of ensuring that food containers are washed at least twice a week, and of using sealed drinkers and hoppers to reduce the likelihood of their contents becoming contaminated with droppings. Regular measures to control parasites, such as spraying to eliminate any risk of red mite becoming established, are also vital; it is very difficult to spot any signs until these almost invisible creatures are well established in the aviary environment.

♦ OPPOSITE
Particular groups of birds are susceptible to different health problems. Feather ailments of various types are relatively common in parrots.

♦ LEFT
Typical signs of generalized illness in a bird are displayed by this canary. Note the ruffled feathers and the inability to perch. Loss of interest in food is also common.

DETECTING ILLNESSES

Birds must be watched very closely for signs of illness. The bird's condition deteriorates rapidly if sickness goes undetected. If it loses its appetite to the point that it is no longer eating, medication has very little opportunity to work successfully. Thankfully, products have been introduced over recent years which provide all the bird's nutritional needs. They can keep a sick or injured individual alive for weeks, greatly enhancing the likelihood of a successful recovery. Advice on using products of this type should be obtained from your avian veterinarian.

The number of veterinarians with experience in this field has grown in the last decade, along with increased interest in the birds. It should not be difficult to find someone in your area with the requisite expertise. An avian

veterinarian will treat illness affecting your stock, and can also help when it comes to sexing birds, and offering preventive health care advice, which can be especially valuable if you have a large collection of birds.

Once established in their quarters, birds are generally very healthy. You are most likely to face health problems in your stock when a number of birds are housed together, rather than as individual pairs on their own.

✦ ABOVE
A green-rumped parrotlet showing abnormally coloured areas of plumage as a result of poor diet.

✦ ABOVE
This parrot suffers from an old injury to its toe, which is causing the nail to grow at an angle. Regular trimming of this nail is essential.

✦ RIGHT
Dirty cages can be hazardous for birds. Both disease and parasites, such as red mite, can spread rapidly in such surroundings.

COPING WITH A SICK BIRD

◆ LEFT
A hospital cage for smaller sick birds, with an adjustable heating system.

◆ BELOW LEFT
Administering medication via the pipette needs to be carried out carefully because of the risk of choking the bird.

◆ BELOW RIGHT
Administering a tablet can be carried out successfully if the bird is adequately restrained.

When confronted with a sick bird, the first thing to do is to remove it from the aviary and transfer it to a warm environment. There are special hospital cages available for this purpose, suitable for smaller birds. For larger species, you will need to invest in an infra-red heat lamp, equipped with a variable heat controller. This should be suspended over the bird's isolation quarters, preferably so there is a temperature gradient across the cage, with one end being warmer than the other. As the bird recovers, it will seek out the cooler area. A reflector around the bulb helps to direct the lamp's rays effectively, while an adjustable controller enables you to lower its heat output, a necessary step in re-acclimatizing the bird.

One of the difficulties of avian medicine is that symptoms are remarkably similar for several illnesses; unravelling the cause can be very difficult, which is a problem when treatment has to be started immediately. In many cases, however, the illness is likely to be caused by a bacterial infection, which will respond well to antibiotic treatment. These drugs are available only on veterinary prescription in the UK, but are easily obtainable elsewhere, in the USA for example, where antibiotic remedies may be sold in pet stores.

When using antibiotics, follow the instructions implicitly and do not stop a course of treatment before the recommended period because, although the bird may appear to have recovered, its condition could deteriorate again. If the surviving bacteria develop a resistance to the antibiotic, further treatment is likely to be unsuccessful.

The most common means of administering antibiotics to birds is via their drinking water, but this is not a particularly reliable method, because you cannot be sure how much a sick individual will drink – it may not consume enough of the medication for the drug to be effective. Avoid offering foods which contain a large percentage of water, such as fruit or greenstuff, so as to encourage the bird to drink the treated water. Place the water alongside the perch if the bird is resting there, rather than on the floor, so that it is within easy reach.

In some cases, especially with larger species, your veterinarian may prefer to give the bird an injection. This can speed its recovery quite dramatically, with subsequent treatment given via the bird's food or drinking water.

It is important not to rush the bird's recovery, once its condition starts to improve. It will almost certainly have lost weight, as reflected by the increased prominence of its breastbone. Do not put the bird back in its aviary until such time as its condition has been restored to normal, or it could suffer a relapse. The weather is important, too – the bird must be gradually re-acclimatized to room temperature and then life outdoors. This may mean that a bird that has been ill will have to remain indoors over the winter, until it can be safely re-acclimatized to outdoor life again in the spring.

EYE PROBLEMS

Swelling and inflammation of the eyes can strike any bird, and although the signs are reasonably clear, it is important to remember that they can be indicative of either a localized or a more serious disorder, such as chlamydiosis. Much depends on the bird's demeanour. If just one eye is affected, it is more likely to be the result of a scratch, particularly if the bird appears to be lively and alert and is eating normally. Should both eyes be affected, however, and the bird becomes progressively more depressed, the likelihood is that it is suffering from a more serious illness.

In localized cases, treatment using special ophthalmic ointment or drops

◆ LEFT
Eye problems can develop quickly and require urgent treatment. It is possible that they are indicative of a more general illness, rather than being the result of localized infection or injury.

should be adequate to resolve the condition rapidly. Be prepared to apply the treatment at least four times daily. Reapplication is necessary because

inflammation causes the eye to water, and this will wash out the medication.

It may be easier to apply drops rather than ointment, but you must ensure that the drops are not lost by the bird blinking at the wrong moment. With ointment, smear it out of the tube along the eye, and be sure that it reaches its target. Hold the bird for a few minutes afterwards so that the ointment can dissolve in the tear fluid, or the bird may wipe it off on to a convenient perch as soon as it is returned to its quarters. Recovery in most cases of this type is rapid, and the inflammation soon subsides, but do not cease treatment prematurely.

Try to identify the cause of the problem if you have several birds in one aviary affected by eye ailments. It might be, for example, that the perches are dirty, and by rubbing their heads on the sides of the perches, the birds are acquiring an infection. The problem may also be linked with the diet: a shortage of Vitamin A can trigger eye problems. Cataracts will develop on occasion in birds with red eyes, and will also occur in elderly parrots. Other eye problems are relatively rare in pet or aviary birds.

1 A white-breasted kingfisher afflicted by an eye ailment. Seek experienced veterinary advice to obtain the correct diagnosis at the outset.

2 Apply treatment carefully to prevent the medication missing its target, in the case of drops, or being wiped off immediately.

3 Holding the patient for a few moments after the treatment will allow the medication to start dissolving into the eye fluid.

4 Provided that the bird can see well out of one eye, and the problem is localized, then it should continue to eat normally.

VIRUSES

Bacterial illnesses can be controlled by means of antibiotics, but this group of drugs is ineffective against viruses. The most serious viral illnesses encountered in aviary birds affect the plumage of parrots. French moult was first recorded in the huge breeding establishments set up in the late 1800s, and can be devastating in its effects. It afflicts young budgerigars at the age of four weeks or so, and results in the loss of flight and tail feathers. Some birds are affected much more severely than others, to the extent that they cannot fly.

There is nothing that can be done by way of treatment. Chicks suffering from French moult should be homed as pets, rather than kept for breeding purposes. In a number of cases, they will regrow their missing feathers, but they may retain tell-tale signs, such as traces of dried blood in the feather shaft, close to the skin.

Good hygiene is important in preventing the spread of this illness. Do not clean nest boxes with the same brush because this can transmit the

virus, and wash concaves (wooden blocks hollowed out at one end, used in budgerigars' next boxes) in disinfectant. The virus spreads easily through feather dust.

The other serious viral ailment encountered in aviculture is psittacine beak and feather disease (PBFD). This was first recognized in cockatoos, but it has now spread to many types of parrot. Affected birds show loss of feathering, with the tissue of their bills becoming soft and overgrown. The claws, too, are affected in a similar way. The depressive effect of this virus

on the immune system means that the bird will succumb to other infections as its condition deteriorates over the course of several months.

Although there is no treatment available as yet, there is a diagnostic test which enables sufferers from PBFD to be identified early. The condition in its early stages can be confused with feather plucking. Affected birds must be kept strictly on their own because they represent a serious threat to the health of others. The PBFD virus also spreads easily through feather dust.

♦ LEFT
French moult in budgerigars. Note the absence of the flight feathers along the back edge of the wings, and the missing tail feathers. Milder cases will sometimes recover spontaneously.

♦ RIGHT
Similar illnesses to French moult have been recorded in parrots, both in wild and captive stock, but are less common. This is an affected Adelaide rosella.

INJURIES

◆ BELOW
The bill of this Indian ring-necked parakeet has been badly damaged. In some cases, artificial bills are fitted, enabling the bird to eat properly.

Unfortunately, there is always a possibility that injuries will arise, both within the confines of the home and in aviary surroundings outdoors, and you need to take adequate precautions to minimize the risks. You also need to be aware of what to do and who to contact when an injury does occur. The outcome may otherwise prove fatal, or could leave the bird permanently handicapped.

One of the most common injuries occurs when a bird flies into an obstruction, such as a pane of glass in the home, or even the mesh of the aviary flight, in the case of young Australian parakeets, which are especially nervous when they first leave the nest.

With this type of injury, the affected individual is likely to end up stunned and disorientated on the floor. There may be no immediate sign of the collision on the bird's body, but if you look closely at the area of the cere, above the bill, you may notice a slight sign of impact here, particularly if the bird collided with mesh. It is impossible to treat this condition but, if transferred to quiet, darkened

surroundings, the bird should recover uneventfully on its own. Occasionally, however, the skull may have been fractured and there could be an underlying brain haemorrhage. In almost all cases this will prove fatal.

Where birds are being housed in adjoining flights, it is vital that both sides of the panel separating them are clad with mesh, as this should create a barrier which prevents neighbouring pairs from coming into contact with each other. Even so, you should check the panel at regular intervals, because the mesh can sag, allowing the birds direct contact. This in turn can lead to badly bitten toes. If necessary, you can slide wooden spacers in between the mesh to keep the panel sheets

apart. The treatment of fighting injuries in birds depends greatly on their severity. Stemming blood flow has to be the first priority, after which the bird should be left in a quiet and darkened area to recover from the shock. An electrolyte solution can also be helpful in such cases.

Fighting between neighbouring birds can also result in bill injuries. This may have serious consequences for the bird's appearance, and it emphasizes the need to check the double-wiring in the flight at regular intervals. Bill injuries can also arise as the result of displays of aggression between birds sharing an aviary – notably cockatoos, where cocks can launch into sudden, vicious attacks on their would-be mates on occasions.

With an injury of this type, handling must again be kept to a minimum because it may exacerbate the effects of shock. You may need to do no more than stem the blood flow by pressing on the damaged part of the bill, particularly the central area in the case of the upper beak.

The advice of a specialist avian vet should be sought, to ascertain the best

TRIMMING THE CLAWS OF A NORWICH CANARY

1 Overgrown claws are hazardous. Birds can become caught up in their quarters, or breeding pairs may drag chicks out of the nest.

2 Use special nail clippers. Trimming is carried out at the start of the breeding season, when the birds are moved to breeding cages.

3 Carry out clipping in a good light, so as not to cut the nails too short and cause them to bleed. Take particular care with dark nails.

way of treating the injury in the longer term. Initially, however, a diet of softfood is likely to be needed, so that the bird can continue feeding. The injury will be painful, and the bird is unlikely to be able to crack either seeds or a complete diet.

So long as the bird can be kept alive through this critical early phase after injury, and depending on how badly the bill has been damaged, it is possible that the tissue will regrow. This is usually a slow process, and the bill is unlikely to reach its full length again. Even so, the regrowth should be adequate to allow the bird to eat hard foods again in due course. Some reshaping of the bill may be needed to improve the bird's appearance once the bill starts to regrow. Reshaping of the bill should be undertaken by an avian vet.

Modern veterinary materials mean that in certain cases where the bill has been badly injured, it may be possible for a false bill to be fitted, even on a temporary basis. The false bill should function almost as effectively as the original. This type of surgery is highly skilled however, and may not be advisable in all cases.

Fractures of the limbs are quite unusual in aviary birds, but should be suspected in cases where a bird suddenly appears to have difficulty in perching or flying. Treatment may involve immobilizing the injured area; the degree of function which returns after treatment depends in part on the site of the fracture. An X-ray assessment will usually give the best insight into the extent of the damage.

In cases where fighting has occurred and the bird has suffered a loss of feathers and skin trauma,

REPAIRING A LOVEBIRD CHICK'S LEG

1 Pictured are the legs of a lovebird chick, which have become splayed in the nest. If they are not treated, the bird will be unable to perch properly.

2 There are various techniques which can be used, and an experienced avian vet will be able to give you the best advice on what to do.

3 By effectively shackling the legs together, the weakened legs are strengthened. They will now carry the bird's weight even when it is mature.

4 Care must be taken not to constrict the blood flow to either limb. Check that the string is not so tight that it cuts into the bird's flesh.

healing should occur naturally without too many problems. Birds rarely develop abscesses, unlike mammals, although bruising, which causes the skin to turn a deep shade of purple, is often associated with this type of injury. Bruising will usually fade after a few days. Lost feathers will be replaced almost immediately, emerging as spikes at first before unfurling.

Provided that the injury is superficial, healing should leave no lasting damage. Even so, do not reintroduce the bird to its mate as soon as it appears to have recovered because it is likely to be attacked

again. Instead, introduce the pair on neutral territory. In the case of parrots, once one bird has turned on its partner, do not reintroduce them; fighting can occur again, and this time the outcome could be fatal. With other birds, such as pigeons and doves, it may be possible to reintroduce pairs successfully before the end of the breeding season, but make changes to the aviary decor first. Providing more cover will help, because it could be that the hen did not feel sufficiently secure in her quarters to start nesting. This will also give the hen more protection from her mate.

PARASITES

The most common health problems encountered by bird-keepers come from parasitic ailments. For this reason it is extremely important to screen or treat newly acquired stock before adding them to an existing collection. Parasites multiply very rapidly in favourable conditions, while their small size and inconspicuous nature means their presence can be easily overlooked until they are posing a serious health risk. Young birds are generally most vulnerable. Parasites can be broadly sub-divided into two categories – external and internal.

EXTERNAL PARASITES

Mites and lice are the most commonly encountered external parasites in aviary stock. Red mites (*Dermanyssus gallinae*) are relatively common and have an unusual life cycle that makes them difficult to eliminate, particularly once they become established in birdroom surroundings. These mites spend only part of their time on the hosts, emerging under cover of darkness to suck the blood of the birds. Then they retreat to their hiding places – cracks in the corners of cages or other nooks and crannies. Red mites present a particular hazard during the breeding season because they live in nest boxes and nesting pans, sucking the blood of adult birds and chicks, which gives them their characteristic coloration.

They are capable of living for months without feeding, so they can survive from one breeding season to the next, with their numbers growing even more rapidly during the following year. Severe infestations can cause anaemia in the chicks, stunting their growth, and may even prove fatal. In addition, red mites are capable of transmitting microscopic blood parasites when they feed, which can also be very harmful.

The other mite of concern is the scaly-face mite (*Knemidocoptes*), which is most commonly seen in budgerigars, although some other birds, notably kakarikis, are vulnerable to it as well. It spreads readily from bird to bird by direct contact, and may also be picked up off the perches, as the bird wipes its bill in a bid to relieve the irritation. The earliest signs of scaly face are tiny snail-like tracks across the upper bill, with more obvious crusty swellings developing around the side of the bill, the cere and sometimes elsewhere on the body as well. In canaries, the legs are often invaded by these parasites, causing them to have an unhealthy, swollen and crusty appearance.

Treatment is straightforward, although it will be necessary to remove affected birds from the aviary until they have recovered. It is also a good idea to scrub off or replace the perches, to contain the spread of the mites. Traditional proprietary remedies to be applied to the affected areas are available from pet stores. Petroleum jelly can be equally effective, blocking off the breathing tubes of the mites. An application of ivermectin, in drop form, to the skin at the back of the neck from where it is absorbed into the body, can kill these mites very efficiently. Only one rather than

♦ LEFT
It is advisable to treat all new arrivals for parasites before allowing them into aviary surroundings. Here a cockatiel is being sprayed with a special aerosol to kill off any mites or lice.

TO PREVENT RED MITE INFESTATIONS

● Treat all new birds with a special red mite medication.

● Start out with new rather than secondhand equipment.

● Use special mite-killing preparations to wash out nest boxes and breeding cages.

● Discourage wild birds from landing on the aviary, because they are often infested with the parasites and can easily transmit them to aviary occupants.

◆ BELOW
Scaly face in a budgerigar. This disfiguring
parasitic ailment must be treated as early as
possible; otherwise the mites may spread
around the eyes.

◆ BELOW
Scaly face in a budgerigar. This disfiguring
parasitic ailment must be treated as early as
possible; otherwise the mites may spread
around the eyes.

◆ BELOW
A sample of droppings can reveal much
about a bird's overall state of health. This
roundworm has been passed out with
the droppings.

regular applications will be needed,
but contact your veterinarian about
this method of treatment. The correct
dosage is critical for the bird's safety.

Lice, visible as thin dark streaks,
often on the wings, represent far less
of a problem than mites. They spend
their whole life cycle on their host,
and are spread by close contact in a
nest or roosting site. Treatment as
for red mite will kill these parasites.
Untreated, they may result in tatty,
frayed feathering. Affected individuals
will be seen to preen themselves far
more than usual.

INTERNAL PARASITES

Microscopic unicellular organisms
called protozoa can cause serious
ill-health in birds; pigeons, doves and
budgerigars are especially vulnerable
to the effects of *Trichomonas*
protozoa. These multiply in the
crop, causing it to swell with gas,
and preventing the bird from eating
properly. Affected budgerigars will
spend longer than usual at their seed
hopper or food pot, and appear to eat.
On close inspection, you will see that
the seed has not been swallowed, only
dehusked; dark pieces of canary seed
in the food pot are a tell-tale sign.

Treatment consists of emptying the
crop gently, by holding the bird upside
down and milking the gas out,
massaging the crop in the direction of
the head. Specific medication to treat
trichomoniasis can be obtained from
a veterinarian.

The infestation can spread quite
widely through a colony before signs
become apparent. Young chicks are
vulnerable soon after fledging; they
lose weight rapidly and fade away. It is
a good idea to treat all the birds in an
aviary when a case of trichomoniasis
occurs because there are almost
certainly others carrying the infection,
and further outbreaks are likely.

Pheasants and quails are at risk
from similar protozoa affecting
the digestive tract, resulting

◆ RIGHT
The risk of parasitic illnesses
occuring is much reduced in clean
and hygienic aviary surroundings.
This is one area of bird care where
hard work really does pay off.

in severe and sometimes blood-stained
diarrhoea. Examination of a fresh
sample of droppings should serve
to identify the actual cause of the
infection, often called coccidosis after
the name of the microbe concerned.
Aside from treatment, thorough
disinfection of the birds' surroundings
will be needed to avoid reinfection.

Intestinal worms pose a serious
health problem, and preventive
treatment prior to releasing the
birds into aviary surroundings is
recommended. If the parasites become
established in the environment, it will
be almost impossible to eliminate
them successfully.

Roundworms are like small white
earthworms in appearance, as opposed
to tapeworms, which have a flattened
body shape. Both release thousands of
eggs into the bird's quarters, but there
is a key difference between them in
terms of their subsequent
development. After a few days,
roundworm eggs will represent a
hazard to birds that come into contact
with them, whereas tapeworm eggs
must be eaten by an invertebrate first.

FEATHER PLUCKING

This disorder is a particular problem in the case of pet parrots. Unfortunately, there is no single cause; various factors may be involved, including boredom, an inadequate diet and lack of opportunity to bathe. This may be the most significant factor – the plumage becomes dry and will not lie flat, which may in turn encourage the parrot to remove its feathers as it becomes frustrated attempting to keep them in place.

Prevention is much easier than cure, particularly as once this problem arises, it can soon become habitual. There are deterrent sprays that you can use in an attempt to persuade the parrot to desist from this behaviour, but they are rarely successful. Changing the bird's environment can be just as effective. It is always worth using a spray to kill mites and lice, though, just in case parasites of this type are causing underlying irritation which has triggered the feather plucking. Seeking the advice of an experienced avian veterinarian may help to isolate the problem rapidly.

With finches and softbills, feather plucking is far less common, especially among established birds. If it does occur, it can be indicative of overcrowding, and once the birds are housed in spacious surroundings, the feathers will regrow without any further problem.

Feather-plucking is less common when parrots are housed in outdoor aviaries, although it may occur on occasion, and can often be linked with the hen's desire to go to nest. Hen Abyssinian lovebirds may pluck their feathers to use as a nest lining, but this is not a matter for concern – these feathers will soon regrow.

◆ LEFT
African grey parrots are especially vulnerable to plucking their feathers, typically on the breast and abdomen, as in this case. It can be very difficult to correct this behaviour.

Where feather-plucking is much more problematic is in the case of young chicks being plucked by their parents while they are still in the nest. This abnormal behaviour is most common in budgerigars and lutino cockatiels, as well as some lories and lorikeets. There is clear evidence that feather-plucking of this type is inherited, at least in some cases. Transferring the eggs of pairs known to pluck their offspring to those which do not is likely to result in the chicks being reared normally. Unfortunately, when these fostered birds are paired up as adults, the vice will re-emerge, and they will pluck their chicks.

It is sometimes possible to break this cycle, by using a special spray designed for the purpose, applying it when the chicks are at their most vulnerable, with their feathers emerging over the neck and shoulder area. Provided that you can deter the adult birds at this stage, there is a chance that the chicks will emerge from the nest with their feathering intact. Assuming this does prove successful, you will still need to treat future chicks in the same way.

When chicks emerge from the nest badly plucked, keep watch on them to ensure that they do not become chilled. The only other solution, aside from fostering, is to remove the chicks as their feathers start to emerge, and complete the rearing process by hand, to prevent feather-plucking occurring.

TUMOURS

These growths are not a common problem in most birds, with the notable exception of budgerigars, where they typically afflict about one in three. Tumours can be divided into two categories – benign (non-cancerous) and malignant. Benign tumours are usually fairly superficial. Pet budgerigars often suffer from fatty lumps of this type, known as lipomas, that appear on or near the breastbone. These can be removed surgically while they are still relatively small, although unfortunately they often recur and, as they become larger, interfere with the bird's ability to fly properly.

Internal tumours of the body organs are harder to detect. Weight loss and a change in cere coloration, in the case of the budgerigar, are typical signs, with the reproductive organs and kidneys being common sites for the growths. There is usually little that can be done.

The cause of such tumours is unclear, although it has been suggested that a virus could be implicated. Up to a third of budgerigars will develop a tumour at some stage in their lives, and although most strike middle-aged or elderly birds, such growths can develop in birds as young as 18 months, and are a common cause of death, especially in pet birds.

One type of tumour which is known to be caused by a virus is a papilloma. This is a particular problem in the larger parrots, especially in macaws and Amazons. Papillomas, with their distinctive wart-like appearance, are most obvious when they occur around the eyes, but they can also develop within the cloaca, which lies inside the vent; in such cases the tumour may have been sexually transmitted.

The first obvious indication of this condition, which is known as cloacal papillomatosis, is the emergence of the papilloma through the vent, or possibly unexplained blood loss on the floor of the parrot's quarters. Other symptoms may include constipation and blood-stained droppings, because of the delicate nature of cloacal papillomas, which bleed readily.

The link between papillomas on the head and in the vent is the result of the fact that pairs of parrots engage in vent preening prior to mating, so that the virus spreads between these parts of the body as a result. Surgery to cut out cloacal papillomas is not recommended, because of the risk of severe blood loss, so a technique known as cryosurgery is often used. The bird is anaesthetized and the tumour is frozen and killed with liquid nitrogen, ultimately sloughing off out of the vent. Another approach which has proved successful is for an avian vet to make a vaccine, which is given to the parrot. The vaccine stimulates the bird's immune system enough to kill the tumour.

♦ LEFT
A budgerigar with a lipoma. These fatty tumours are quite common, especially in heavier-type pet birds. The tumour has a distinctive yellowish appearance.

THE SHOW SCENE

Details of bird shows can be found in the bird-keeping magazines and club newsletters. These may vary from small-scale local events to regional and national shows. Some cater for one particular type of bird, such as budgerigars, and some have classes for a variety of species. Even if you are not exhibiting, it is worth visiting a show. It will give you an insight into what is required to exhibit birds successfully, as well as enabling you to meet fellow fanciers and to learn more about the birds on view.

Judging standards differ according to the type of bird. As a general rule, condition is important – birds that are moulting will not do well at a show. For those species that have been selectively bred and have a number of colour varieties, such as the budgerigar or zebra finch, there are official judging standards. These specify what constitutes ideal appearance or "type" in exhibitor's parlance – coloration and markings among other things – with points awarded under different headings. The birds in a class are not being judged against each other, but against the ideal established for the variety concerned.

For those species without an official standard, including most finches and softbills, condition is the prime concern. Missing nails, for example, will mean lost points.

♦ OPPOSITE
Judging canaries at a show. These birds are assessed according to the breed standard, with the judge marking each bird against the ideal, rather than against the other entries in the class.

♦ LEFT
A considerable amount of time and commitment is necessary when it comes to successful showing. The birds must be properly trained for such events, and must be able to settle happily in their cages.

ENTERING A SHOW

Much depends on the type of birds you are intending to exhibit. For those with judging standards, acquire stock from a reputable breeder. You are unlikely to find suitable birds in your local pet store. When setting out to establish an exhibition stud, quality is far more significant than quantity. It is always better to buy two pairs of good-quality birds than ten birds of a more mediocre quality. The cost of acquiring exhibition stock depends on not only the type of bird, but also the breeder's reputation – those who are doing well on the show bench are likely to charge correspondingly more for their birds. Budgerigars and certain canary varieties are among the most expensive, whereas top-quality examples of finches, such as Bengalese (society finches), are relatively inexpensive by way of comparison.

Join the relevant national society. Through this organization you will be able to enter your birds in the widest possible range of classes at a show. You will also receive a variety of publications giving details of the major show events.

Show cages are another essential purchase, especially for those varieties that are judged to specific standards. The idea is that the cages should all be the same so that judges are not distracted by the housing of the exhibit. It is vital to have the right type of show cage for the breed concerned. For instance, budgerigars are all exhibited in cages with white interiors and black exteriors. When several birds are exhibited together in "teams", the basic design is scaled up from that used for a single bird. Budgerigars and canaries are usually exhibited individually, whereas pairs of finches are more commonly shown. A good pair will always win over a single bird, simply because it is harder to stage a pair in top condition.

WHAT TO TAKE
Carrying case for bird cages
Water containers as necessary
Directions to the show venue
Paperwork for the show
Mobile phone in case of breakdown
Camera to photograph the winners
Carrying box in case you buy birds

◆ LEFT
Details of shows are normally advertised in the bird-keeping press. Larger events will typically attract thousands of entries.

◆ OPPOSITE
BOTTOM RIGHT
Birds travel better in the dark, and because they are less prone to panic, there is less chance they will damage their plumage.

◆ OPPOSITE
BOTTOM LEFT
A carrying box will be useful if you wish to buy any birds at the show.

TRIMMING THE MASK OF A BUDGERIGAR

1 Exhibition budgerigars often have overlapping spots on their faces, when in fact there should only be three on each side.

2 Trimming the mask calls for patience and skill: mistakes can ruin the bird's exhibition potential. Work slowly around the bird's face.

3 A pair of tweezers will allow you to pull out the overlapping feathers one at a time, making it easier to create the symmetrical pattern of spots.

4 Here is the finished result. The loss of the odd feather causes the budgerigar no discomfort. The feathers will regrow in time.

◆ ABOVE
A typical exhibition budgerigar with a trimmed mask. Take care not to damage other feathering when you catch and restrain the bird for the purpose of mask trimming.

No decor is allowed in the show cages, with the notable exception of softbill classes. The aim, in this case, is to devise a natural backdrop which complements the appearance of the bird or birds. Smaller softbills may be shown in pairs. A variety of materials, such as moss, bark and even exotic flowers, may be incorporated and, although a good backdrop display will not win the class, it can make the difference when two entries are otherwise inseparable.

GOOD PREPARATION
Getting birds ready for a show is an art because they need to be in peak condition for the event. Should they start to moult or even damage a feather, this will effectively ruin their chances. Regular spraying can help with the conditioning process. Special conditioners may be added to the spray to help develop a healthy gloss on the plumage.

There are no shortcuts to obtaining show success. If a bird is not in top condition, then it will not win, which is often why a winner at one show may end up being unplaced at another.

SHOWING

Having decided to enter a show, the first step is to write to the show secretary for the schedule, which will set out the different classes, and an entry form. Enclose a stamped, self-addressed envelope. Read the schedule very carefully alongside the entry form. If you make a mistake at this stage and enter your birds in the wrong class, they will be disqualified on the day and you will lose your entry fee. Return the completed entry form with payment as soon as possible, to be certain that it arrives before the closing date for entries.

A week prior to the show, check and clean the show cages. They should be in good condition for the show – restore any chipped paintwork, for example – because any damage may spoil your bird's chances of winning if it is up against a bird of equal merit in an immaculate cage.

Assess your bird's condition carefully as the time for the show approaches. Some budgerigars may need their mask trimmed, and you should do this a few days beforehand, taking great care not to damage the plumage when holding the bird.

◆ ABOVE
It is not simply a matter of catching your entries before the event. These Norwich fancy canaries are being trained with a show cage.

◆ BELOW LEFT
Watering of exhibits usually takes place after judging, so the birds cannot wet their plumage.

◆ BELOW RIGHT
Standard show cages mean that the judges are not distracted by the bird housing. The numbers on the cages identify the exhibits.

On the morning of the show, allow yourself plenty of time to reach the venue, particularly if you do not know the area. Remember to allow extra time for parking. Arriving early means that the birds will have time to settle down on the show bench before judging takes place, which is likely to improve their chances; agitated birds rarely look their best.

◆ BELOW
Stewards work alongside the judge, giving them an excellent opportunity to gain insight into the features which the judges are looking for in competitions.

◆ BELOW
Although official judging standards exist for many birds, other birds, such as this lineolated parakeet, are judged on the basis of their feather condition and steadiness.

Judging is carried out in most cases without an audience. If you want to see what is involved, volunteer to be a show steward. Those birds that are relatively tame and used to human contact will often show to best effect, simply because they will not retreat to the floor of the cage out of fear, when they are inspected by the judge at close quarters.

One of the more unusual aspects of showing birds is that a winning bird at one event may not even be placed at its next show. This is usually due to the bird's condition. So although purchasing other people's winning birds (usually at highly inflated prices) may seem like a good way to instant show success, in fact, consistent winners are those who pay attention

to detail, constantly seeking to improve the type of their birds by careful pairings. Whether or not your birds win, try not to lose sight of the fact that exhibiting is meant to be enjoyable, irrespective of the outcome. There is always the next event to look forward to, and there is every possibility that your birds could win a class there.

◆ RIGHT
Birds bred for their appearance or "type" are housed in plain cages, while many softbills are typically displayed for show purposes in decorated cages. The aim of the decor is to complement the bird's appearance.

SHOW PLANNING

The judging of birds can be a difficult task, and so much depends on the co-operation of the exhibits themselves. If a bird skulks on the floor of its show cage and refuses to co-operate with the judging process, it will be impossible to assess its potential and it will not score highly.

The best exhibitors are those who train their birds properly from an early age, so that the birds are used to being accommodated in show cages, with humans close to them. In the case of young budgerigars, this process may begin when the chicks are still in the nest; handling at this stage means that the birds will be finger-tame by the time they emerge from the nest.

Deciding which of the birds in your collection will be good enough to win at shows in the future can be very difficult. This is particularly true of youngsters, as their full potential may not be apparent until they are older. As a result, many exhibition breeders retain the majority of their young stock until they have moulted out,

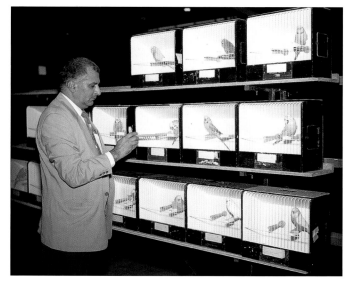

♦ ABOVE
Although a trained show budgerigar will move from perch to perch, the use of a judging stick will help the judge gain a better overall impression.

♦ BELOW
Judges are only able to assess the birds for the short time they are put in front of them.

housing them in spacious flights where they can continue their development once independent. Regular training sessions at this stage will allow the birds to become used to their show cages.

Shows often hold classes for young birds, and these will allow you to test the show potential of your chicks, under the neutral eye of a judge. Even so, do not necessarily part with birds which fail to be placed at a handful of shows – it is also important to bear in mind their pedigree. Quality has a way of coming to the fore, and if for example, you have a hen bred from the best birds in your stud, who is not herself a top-ranked show bird, she could still make a contribution to the development of your stud. Champion exhibitors often breed their best birds not necessarily from their best show birds, but from closely-related individuals. Also, it can be especially

♦ RIGHT
A thorough understanding of the desirable characteristics of a particular bird variety are essential for the judge.

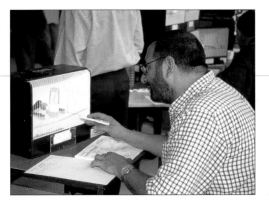

difficult to acquire good quality hens, compared with cocks; you should always think carefully before disposing of a hen bird.

Once you have a bird which is doing well on the show bench, and is winning regularly, do not be tempted to enter it in as many events as possible. Birds need to rest after a show, and over-showing may adversely affect their breeding performance.

Lists of all shows – local, regional and national – are usually published around the start of the show season in

the bird-keeping press, and it is a good idea to plan out well in advance which shows you want to attend, and even which birds you want to enter in particular events. Bear in mind that the

♦ BELOW
At larger shows, class winners are judged to find the best of breed, then breed winners are judged to find the best of group. The winners will compete for the best-in-show award.

birds you select at this stage may not be in top condition by the time of the show however, and that adjustments in your plans prior to some shows will be inevitable.

BREEDING BIRDS

The start of the breeding period is always exciting, as the birds start nesting. Some birds are easier to breed than others, partly because they can be sexed visually at the outset, although there are now reliable scientific methods of determining the gender of birds where both sexes are identical in appearance. It is important to make the necessary preparations for the breeding period well in advance, in terms of ensuring that the birds are paired up properly. It can actually be surprisingly difficult obtaining hen canaries, for example, right at the start of the nesting period, and following a move at this stage, they may also have little or no interest in breeding in strange surroundings.

You need to discover as much as possible about the breeding habits of the birds which you are keeping, to ensure that you offer them suitable nesting facilities. While parrots generally need a nestbox, softbills in particular vary quite widely in their nesting requirements. Some, such as starlings and mynahs, will use a nestbox, whereas others, such as sunbirds, will need suitable material and an environment where they can construct their own nest.

+ OPPOSITE
The likelihood of successful breeding with finches and softbills, such as this green tanager, will be enhanced if the birds are housed in planted aviaries.

+ LEFT
It is a rewarding time when chicks have hatched, but it is important not to disturb the adult birds, especially if breeding for the first time, as they may be nervous.

THE BREEDING SEASON

◆ BELOW
The age of sexual maturity differs between the species. These young Gouldian finches will be ready to breed within a year, but larger parrots can take more than five years to mature.

Today, successful breeding of many species has become commonplace, because of advances in incubator technology and the development of commercial hand-rearing diets. Parrots in particular are now being raised on a wider scale than ever before. Nevertheless, there are pitfalls along the path to success, and patience is necessary. It can take at least one year after a move – and perhaps four or five in the case of the larger parrots – for birds to settle down to breed.

At the outset, offer breeding birds a range of nesting options. Many parrots will refuse to breed in the open part of the flight, preferring the

◆ BELOW
The age of sexual maturity differs between the species. These young Gouldian finches will be ready to breed within a year, but larger parrots can take more than five years to mature.

◆ ABOVE
Birds such as this orange-winged Amazon cannot be sexed visually.

seclusion offered by the shelter. Finches and softbills, too, will show individual preferences when it comes to nesting. It may be possible to persuade them to use a nest box or a platform as a support for their nests, but often they prefer to construct their own nest in a bush. This can be risky because the structure might collapse, with eggs or even chicks being lost as a consequence.

Should you be interested in breeding colour varieties, you will need to house your birds in individual pairs, to ensure the parentage of the chicks. Breeding cages can be used for most of the smaller species but you will need a block of aviaries for larger birds, including parrots and parakeets.

Preparing well in advance for the breeding season will give you the greatest likelihood of success. In the case of breeding cages and nest boxes which have been used before, wash these out with a special safe avian

product to kill any parasites, especially red mites. Rinse out the cages and boxes and allow them to dry before reassembling. Inspect nest boxes provided for parrots for any signs of damage, carrying out any repairs as necessary. Check that the ladder in the interior has not become weakened by the birds gnawing at the sides of the box. Should this fall down at a later stage, making it hard to reach the bottom of the nesting cavity, it could result in the loss of eggs or chicks.

NEW BIRD STOCK

In most cases, it will not be until the following year that the birds will have settled down sufficiently in their new aviary to start breeding, but in the case of the more prolific species, such as budgerigars, cockatiels and zebra finches, for example, they will often start nesting quite soon after a move, particularly if this occurs in the early spring.

Parrots, including budgerigars, will generally use a nest box for breeding purposes, or sometimes a hollow log. They rarely build any sort of nest within the box.

It can be helpful if the nest box is assembled with screws because you will then be able to replace one of the sides if this has been damaged by the birds' bills. If a hole develops here prior to egg-laying, the extra light entering through the gap may be sufficient to stop the hen from using the box; after egg-laying, there is a risk that eggs or chicks could be lost through the gap. Trying to carry out repairs when the box is occupied may cause the birds to abandon the nest.

A BALANCED DIET

Particular attention also needs to be paid to the birds' diet prior to the breeding season. A good diet can encourage breeding activity, and will help to ensure that the chicks receive the right nutritional balance to meet their growth requirements, and increase their chances of survival.

Soaked seed is valuable for seed-eaters, including parrots, at this time, and will raise the protein level of their diet if they are not fed a complete diet. Softening the seed improves its digestibility for young birds, and if the adults are used to this food, they will continue to eat it and in turn will feed it to their chicks. The same applies in the case of softfoods, such as egg food, which is widely used by canary breeders.

Calcium is of great importance to breeding birds, since it is the key component of eggshells. Because seed is deficient in calcium, seed-eating birds should have access to cuttlefish bone or a calcium block throughout the year. The drain on the hen's body may be too severe if calcium is only available during the breeding period.

Most softbills will obtain adequate calcium through their softfood, but highly insectivorous ones are also at risk of suffering a deficiency, because of the unbalanced calcium : phosphorus ratio in livefoods. A soluble calcium supplement is recommended, as is using a nutritional balancer with the livefood. This is important when there are chicks in the nest, otherwise the chicks could suffer from skeletal weakness, in the form of rickets.

◆ LEFT
Finches often prefer to build their own nests, concealing the site in vegetation. On occasions, however, they may adopt a wicker nesting basket or open-fronted nest box.

SEXING BIRDS

◆ BELOW
In many cases, cock birds are more colourful
than hens, but there are exceptions, as with
Ruppell's parrot, which is an African species.

The first stage in breeding birds
successfully is to obtain a male and
female. This is straightforward in
some cases – budgerigars for example,
where there is a clear visual means of
separating the sexes. In other cases,
however, it can be much more
difficult. With finches such as nuns,

breeders will often obtain a group
of four or six individuals in the hope
of ensuring that they have at least
one pair.

How to determine the gender
of birds when there is no visual
distinction between the sexes is a
long-standing problem. A popular

method from the Victorian era is the
pelvic bone test. Pelvic bones can be
felt just above the vent and become
more widely spaced in hens just prior
to the laying period. Unfortunately,
while this method is very effective at
this stage, it cannot be applied reliably
at other times of the year. By the time

the hen is in breeding condition, of course, other behavioural signs are apparent that enable the sexes to be distinguished. Cocks tend to sing more and display to their mates, while hens are likely to be searching for nesting material, and spending longer in their chosen nest site.

During the 1980s, bird-keepers concentrated on attempting to find ways of sexing large birds. This is particularly important in the case of parrots, where two birds may behave as a pair, feeding and preening each other, even though they are of the same sex. Surgical sexing, which entails inserting an instrument called an endoscope through the body wall to view the sex organs directly, was favoured at first. It is still useful, but because of the slight risk involved in using anaesthetic, it has tended to fall out of favour.

DNA sexing is now generally the preferred method, partly because it can be used on birds of any age, allowing chicks to be paired successfully, whereas endoscopic sexing requires the birds to be mature in order to give reliable results. A blood sample can be obtained by plucking a suitable feather, which is then dispatched to the laboratory by courier. There is no need to take the bird to a veterinary surgery for this procedure; it can be done at home.

Unfortunately, it is not just a matter of having a male and a female for breeding success, particularly in the case of the larger parrots. Compatibility is a vital factor. This is why proven pairs are more expensive than sexed pairs. By watching the birds closely, you may be able to see if they are compatible, interacting in a friendly way by perching close together and following each other around the aviary.

Even so, especially in the case of two parrots which have been housed together for a period of time, behaviour patterns can often be misleading. Behaviour is much more significant in the case of a group housed together, where there is a choice of partners available; here, matching up a pair can be a matter of trial and error. Mutual preening, feeding and even attempts at mating do not necessarily signify a true pair. If both birds spend long periods of time in the nest box, but no eggs are actually laid, then the likelihood is that the supposed pair is actually comprised of two cock birds. Conversely, if a relatively large number of eggs are laid, which prove to be infertile, then it is probable that you have two hens.

The difficulty of distinguishing pairs in the case of finches is less significant, generally because they can be housed together and allowed to pair off on their own.

As the time for the nesting period approaches, so more obvious behavioural signs – such as the song of the cock bird – will enable you to separate the sexes more easily. If the birds can be caught with minimal disturbance, this is a good time to ring the singing cocks with celluloid rings, so that you will be able to identify them easily throughout the year ahead. However, do not attempt to enter the aviary to catch and ring birds if it is well into the season and there are other birds already breeding, as the disturbance might make them frightened, and you could unwittingly cause them to abandon the nests in their distress.

◆ RIGHT
The gender of many finches is only known from their behaviour. However, distinguishing the gender of the cut-throat is straightforward, as only the cock displays the red throat plumage.

NESTING FACILITIES

There is nothing to be lost by offering birds the opportunity to nest soon after a move. A choice of suitable nesting sites is obviously essential, and you will need to match these with the birds' individual nesting needs. With many finches, softbills and ground birds, such as quails, adequate cover in the aviary is very important to provide a sense of security. The vegetation may be used for nest-building by various species, but it is preferable to persuade them to adopt artificial nesting sites if possible. This reduces the risk of pigeons and doves losing eggs or chicks by having their rather flimsy nests collapsing under them. Position the sites so that the nests will not become flooded if there is a fierce summer storm.

A wide range of different types of nest are available, not just from pet stores but also from specialist mail-order suppliers, advertising in the bird-keeping magazines. For finches and softbills, open-fronted nest boxes

of the appropriate size are useful, with a barrier at the front of the box to prevent the contents from falling out. Other popular alternatives for this group of birds are nesting baskets, of which there are various designs and shapes. These can be attached by means of wire loops, whereas the nest

boxes should be screwed in place. It is vital to fix the nesting sites firmly in place, keeping them level as far as possible.

Canary nest pans, which may be used by other related species which build cup-shaped nests, such as serins, should be fixed in place with screws.

✦ ABOVE
A typical box-type breeding cage, with a sliding tray in place. In the case of finches, a wicker nesting basket can be suspended over the upper part of the cage front, whereas for canaries, the nesting pan will need to be screwed on to the back or sides.

✦ LEFT
A well-designed birdroom housing breeding cages for finches. Accurate record-keeping is very important when breeding birds in this way, with details being recorded on each cage and then transferred to a stock register.

1 Trimming the feathering around the vents of cock and hen canaries is often recommended at the start of the breeding season.

2 This procedure helps to ensure successful mating. However, it is safer to use round-nosed scissors, rather than pointed ones.

◆ ABOVE
A canary nestpan, lined with a layer of felt, holding four dummy eggs. These are used to substitute briefly for real eggs, which ensures that the chicks will be of similar age when they eventually hatch.

◆ ABOVE
Some finches are more likely to nest successfully in breeding cages than others. Most Australian finches are bred in this way, whereas waxbills are more commonly kept in aviaries for breeding purposes.

◆ RIGHT
A typical view of breeding cages stacked in a birdroom. These should be firmly supported on staging, as birds will generally not breed well if housed in cages on the floor.

◆ RIGHT
Security is very important for nesting birds.
The nest pan in this case is supported by
branches in the aviary.

◆ RIGHT
Security is very important for nesting birds.
The nest pan in this case is supported by
branches in the aviary.

They are also likely to be occupied by
smaller doves; their larger relatives
should be offered bigger plywood
trays as nesting receptacles.

Parrots require nesting boxes.
Those produced for budgerigars have
a wooden block, hollowed out at one
end, known as a concave. The nest
boxes are equipped with a sliding
inspection hatch at one end, with a
sheet of glass behind to ensure that

◆ LEFT
Some birds construct
free-standing nests
in vegetation.
Bamboo, seen here,
makes a good plant
choice for an aviary
for this reason.

◆ BELOW LEFT
Unconventional
perhaps, but birds
may value the
security provided by
plastic tubing when
selecting a nesting
site in the aviary.

◆ BELOW RIGHT
Offer a variety of
nesting sites, based
on nesting habits, for
the greatest chance
of breeding success.

eggs or chicks will not fall out when
the box is opened. It is important that
the concave fits snugly into the nest
box so there is no risk of young chicks
accidentally slipping down between
the sides of the box and the concave
and getting stuck there.

Nest boxes for other parrots tend
to be of a significantly taller design,
known as the grandfather-clock type.
They are heavy, being made of thick
ply or timber, partly to withstand the
birds' bills; parrots become especially
destructive as the time for breeding
approaches. This means that the boxes
have to be fixed securely, using
brackets to distribute the weight. They
should be positioned fairly close to the

◆ BELOW
A support, in the form of a basket-like
structure, is recommended for pigeons and
doves, which build loose nests that may otherwise
collapse, with the loss of eggs and/or chicks.

top of the aviary, but allow enough
space for the birds to rest on top of
the box, and for you to lift the lid if
necessary to reach inside. A sliding
side-inspection panel that can be
closed securely with a well-oiled bolt
may be preferable.

The birds enter the box by means
of a perch outside the nest hole with a
mesh ladder extending down the
inside. The perch must be fixed
securely in place so there is no risk of
it becoming dislodged, particularly by
the gnawing activities of the adult pair,

◆ ABOVE
Some birds, such as quails, need good ground
cover for nesting purposes, with hens laying in
a scrape in the ground, often under a bush.

◆ BELOW
Encourage birds to use an accessible part of the
aviary for nest-building. These fruit doves have
chosen a spot that will make inspection difficult.

◆ LEFT
It is important to provide the birds with a
choice of nesting material for them to construct
an adequate nest. Some will build elaborate
structures, lining the interior with feathers.

the base of the pan. A special powder
to kill mites may be sprinkled on the
undersurface first. Loose nesting
material is used to build the nest
itself – twigs, coconut fibre (available
commercially) and dried moss. This
will also be used by other birds.
Pheasant and quail hens, however,
will simply lay in a hollow scrape
in the ground, often under a bush,
without using any additional nesting
materials whatsoever.

and blocking off the interior of the
box. Line the nest box with coarse
shavings, as sold for animal bedding.
For larger parrots, place short strips
of wooden battening on the floor of
the nest box, which the adult birds
can whittle away to form their own
nest lining.

A variety of materials can be
purchased for other groups of birds.
Canary nest pans are lined with
circular felt, sewn in through holes in

◆ RIGHT
Dense tussocks of grass
can be very useful in
providing a nest site for
birds which prefer to nest
on the ground.

◆ BELOW
Wicker finch nesting
baskets are available in a
variety of designs, and are
equipped with wire hooks
at the back, so they can be
suspended easily around
the aviary under cover.

The position of nesting sites can
be crucial when it comes to achieving
breeding success. While Australian
parakeets will breed in the flight under
cover, many parrots, especially those
of rainforest origins, will prefer to
use a nest box located in the relative
darkness of the shelter, although pairs
can prove to be highly individual in
this respect. It is important that the
nest will not become flooded when
it rains, however, and it should
preferably be positioned in a sheltered
corner of the flight, so that the eggs
and chicks will be protected from cold
winds. This is important in the case
of birds such as ring-necked parakeets,
which are likely to nest at an early
stage in the spring. Conversely, in hot

◆ BELOW
Offering a variety of nesting materials is the
best way of ensuring the birds can make an
adequate nest. Providing an iodine nibble will
help to supplement the hen's diet at this time.

◆ BELOW
Moss is a valuable nesting material, but this
should be purchased from bird suppliers or pet
stores rather than collected from the wild,
which in some countries is illegal.

climates, it is equally advisable to offer
protection from the heat in the form
of planted foliage.

In a colony aviary, try to provide
nesting sites around the aviary, to
avoid territorial disputes. Don't expect
to be kept up to date with progress:
in a planted flight you may not even
be aware of the fact that a pair have
gone to nest until you hear the chicks.

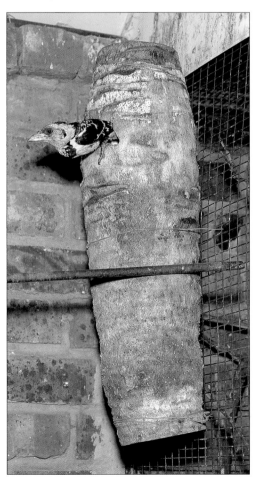

It is not a good idea to probe too
deeply in the vegetation at this time
of year, but simply keep a watch on
the birds from outside the aviary.

Birds are most likely to desert
their nest at the start of the incubation
period if they feel insecure. Do not
disturb them unless you have cause
to suspect that something is wrong.
A sudden fall-off in food consumption
is always a cause for concern, but bear
in mind that in an aviary housing
a number of birds, this may be less
obvious than with a single pair.

◆ ABOVE
Pigeons and doves
share incubation
duties. The cock
birds will occupy the
nest during the day,
with the hen taking
over at night.

◆ RIGHT
Some birds prefer a
deep, natural nesting
site. This Levaillant's
barbet has bored into
an old log to create
its nesting chamber.

SIGNS OF BREEDING ACTIVITY

A number of different signs indicate that breeding activity is likely. Cock birds may become more vocal; cock canaries sing loudly during this period. The cock bird will also be more attentive towards the hen, often chasing her around her quarters and sometimes pausing to try to feed her; this is especially true in the case of parrots. Hens will appear more alert, inspecting possible nesting sites and hunting for suitable nesting material. The pair may become more destructive as well; female budgerigars rip up their sandsheets at this stage, and may become far more territorial than usual. Nest boxes for budgerigars must all be fixed at approximately the same height when they are breeding in a colony together, because otherwise, they are likely to start fighting for possession of the higher boxes. This applies wherever birds of the same species are being housed in a colony.

✦ LEFT
One of the more obvious signs of breeding activity will be increased contact between the members of the pair, with the cock often feeding the hen as a prelude to mating.

✦ BELOW LEFT
Mating will usually occur on a perch, with the hen remaining still while the cock bird hops on to her back. The perches themselves must always be secure, so that the birds can balance without difficulty.

Hens of seed-eating species will nibble more determinedly at the cuttlefish bone in their quarters to raise their calcium intake, which will be vital for the eggshells in due course. Having chosen a nest site, they will spend progressively longer periods of time sitting there, immediately prior to egg-laying. In the case of budgerigars, the increase in the size of the hen's droppings before this event is a warning that the appearance of the eggs is imminent. This is important. Watch the hens carefully at this stage because birds may become egg-bound and require emergency treatment.

In some cases, it is quite easy to tell when the birds are coming into breeding condition because of a

change in their appearance. In the
case of hen budgerigars for example,
their ceres turn a much darker shade
of brown as the time for egg-laying
approaches. Cock golden song
sparrows develop a black bill as they
come into breeding condition, but the
most spectacular colour change is seen
in the case of many of the weavers and
whydahs originating from Africa.
The plumage of cocks of these species
are transformed at the start of the
breeding period. Male whydahs grow
long tail plumes, which are used in
their display, while their weaver
counterparts are temporarily
transformed from their typical rather
dull, sparrow-like appearance into
stunningly beautiful birds.

Out of all birds, however, the
peacock is best-known for its display,
with its magnificent breeding train
taking several years to develop to its
full extent. At the start of the
breeding period, the peacock uses
his magnificent plumes to attract and
maintain his harem of hens and also to
intimidate other males. In the case of
pheasants and quails as well, males can
become very aggressive towards other,
especially as the time for breeding
approaches, and it essential to ensure

they are kept apart, because they will
seriously injure or possibly even kill
each other. Solid partitions between
flights will stop these birds from
attempting to fight through mesh.
You should also regularly check the

double-wiring in adjacent flights
housing parrots, to ensure that any
cock birds cannot reach the toes of
their neighbours, as they too are likely
to become more aggressive at this
stage of the year.

INCUBATION

Assuming all proceeds normally, the eggs should be laid on a daily or, for parrots, alternate day basis. The hen will not start to incubate them immediately. It is quite usual for two or even three eggs to be laid before she starts to incubate them in earnest. This ensures that the chicks hatch at roughly the same time, improving their chances of survival because there will be no age gap between the chicks in the nest.

Canary breeders have capitalized on this, removing the eggs in sequence as they are laid and replacing them with dummy eggs until the fourth morning, when the final egg of the clutch is due to be laid. When assessing the likely date of hatching, based on the incubation period, bear this in mind; the incubation period for the first eggs laid in a clutch is likely to be extended accordingly.

The number of eggs laid in a clutch varies quite widely, ranging from one or two, in the case of pigeons and doves, through to a dozen or more, in the case of pheasants and quails. There may be greater variability in some species than others – budgerigars lay anything from two to eight or

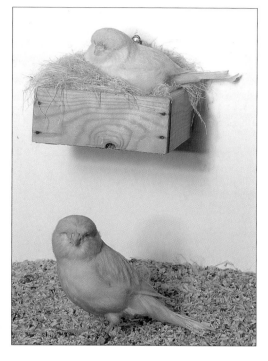

♦ LEFT
A pair of Norwich canaries. Only the hen incubates, but she may not sit tightly on the nest until at least two eggs have been laid. Canaries usually lay four eggs in a clutch.

♦ BELOW LEFT
A pair of citron-crested cockatoos defending their nest box. These and other white cockatoos are unusual amongst parrots in that incubation duties are shared by members of the pair.

♦ BELOW RIGHT
A white-capped pionus parrot hen incubating. Avoid any disturbance: a hen may damage her eggs as she hurriedly tries to leave the box.

more eggs in a clutch. In many species, such as canaries, the hen sits alone, but in others, such as the cockatiels and most cockatoos, incubation duties are synchronized between the pair.

The cock birds will sit for much of the day, with the hen taking over in the late afternoon and remaining on the nest through the night, until the following day.

HATCHING

Once the chicks hatch, you will hear them calling for food, usually as dusk approaches, and you may also see discarded eggshells on the floor of the birds' quarters, often deposited some distance away from the nest itself. Do not disturb the birds unless you suspect that something is seriously wrong; you may cause the nest and chicks to be abandoned, especially with nervous birds such as pigeons and doves, and many finches.

Adjust the birds' food to include more dietary protein at this stage, to meet the growth requirements of the chicks. So strong is the desire for livefood in the form of small, easily digested invertebrates, such as micro-crickets, that other equally nourishing alternatives may be ignored. Waxbills, for example, are unlikely to rear chicks successfully in the absence of livefood, in contrast to the nuns, which are more amenable to rearing foods such as eggfood. This can be obtained from many pet stores, and can usually be offered to the birds straight from the packet, without having to be mixed with water. Scrupulous hygiene is vital at this stage; the young chicks must not be offered sour food.

✦ LEFT
There can be quite a difference in budgerigar chicks when they hatch, as the eggs are laid on alternate days.

✦ BOTTOM RIGHT
As an alternative to using an artificial incubator, broody domestic poultry hens, especially bantams, are sometimes used to hatch the young of similar birds, such as pheasants.

✦ LEFT
Feeding in a dark nest is difficult, so some chicks have light edges to their bills and luminous mouth markings, which help the adult birds find them.

✦ BELOW LEFT
A hatching pheasant. The chicks of ground birds hatch in a more advanced state of development than those which live and nest in trees.

113

HATCHING CANARY CHICKS

1 The eggs of all canaries are speckled, and those of the different breeds cannot be distinguished from each other. Patterns are individual to the eggs.

2 When they hatch, canary chicks are totally dependent on the hen. She will brood them to maintain their body temperature, and feeds them on demand.

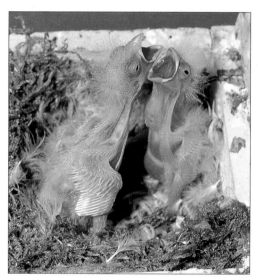

3 These chicks are begging to be fed. Weak or sickly chicks will not be able to lift their heads in this way, and so they will not be fed by the hen.

4 The wide gape of the chicks ensures that they swallow their food. Food passes to the crop of the neck, and the chicks cease begging when this is full.

The young of ground-dwelling species, such as pheasants, hatch in a more advanced state of development than those of tree-nesting birds, but they are still vulnerable, especially if they become wet at any stage. Rearing foods are vital to their well-being.

One of the best ways of monitoring the progress of chicks in the nest is to note the amount of food being consumed. It may be possible to take a quick glance at parrot chicks in the nest, provided that you do not disturb the sitting bird. If it leaves the nest

when you open the aviary, this will provide the ideal opportunity. Putting fresh food in place will distract the adult birds. Following this routine over a number of weeks will ensure that the birds do not become stressed by your presence.

REARING FOODS

The nutritional requirements of all birds will change at different stages of the year, and especially during the breeding season, when their need for protein rises dramatically. The extra protein is needed to meet the growth requirements of their chicks. Young finches, for example, are likely to have left the nest within just a fortnight of hatching, and the adult birds may have reared five chicks, or even more, during this period. As a result, many finches in the wild become highly insectivorous at this stage, and this is reflected by the behaviour of their aviary counterparts. Members of the waxbill group, in common with most softbills, will only rear their chicks if they are provided with an almost constant supply of livefood at this time. Young crickets are ideal for the purpose, being available in different sizes. They are also far more easily digested than mealworms, which can pass through the body of a young chick unaltered, leaving it at serious risk of starvation.

The use of egg food at this time is also recommended, even prior to when the chicks have hatched, so that the adult birds can gain a taste for it. Eggfood is especially popular with canaries, as well as other finches, and is often eaten by softbills and many parrots, such as cockatiels and Australian parakeets. Budgerigars, too, are likely to benefit if this type of food is provided for them when they have young chicks.

Although some bird breeders still mix up their own softfoods to feed to chicks during the rearing period, it is far more commonplace today for packeted recipes to be used, and many of those on the market provide a good nutritional balance. Whichever brand you choose, however, do not change it suddenly during the rearing period, as this can lead to severe digestive upsets in the young birds. Equally, good hygiene is vitally important – clear up any spilt eggfood after each feed, replacing the containers twice daily and washing them with a detergent before rinsing them off thoroughly, drying and refilling.

PREPARING AND GIVING REARING FOODS

1 Mixing up rearing food for canaries. Some foods of this type are available pre-prepared. If adding water, aim for a smooth consistency.

2 As the time for weaning approaches, breeders will often add in blue maw seed, which is a good way to wean the birds on to solid food.

3 Give additional feeds to a young chick in the nest if you suspect that it may not be acquiring sufficient food from its mother.

RINGING

If you want to ring the birds while they are still in the nest, this needs to be carried out when they are a few days old. Generally, only exhibition stock is close-rung in this way, but there may be legal requirements in some countries for native species to be banded as a means of identifying birds bred in captivity.

Ringing can be carried out quite easily. Group the three longest toes together and slide the ring over these, up to the ball of the foot. Then, with the small toe kept parallel and in contact with the leg behind, it should be possible to slide the ring over the toe and up the leg. Check that the ring can move freely up and down the leg. If the chick is too old when you try to ring it, the band will be too small to fit over the ball of its foot, but avoid disturbing the adult birds in the nest any more than is necessary.

Club members usually obtain their rings from the society to which they belong. Ring manufacturers advertise in bird-keeping publications. Split-type rings can be useful for identification purposes – to mark a cock finch that is singing and would be impossible to pick out later in the year, for example. These split rings clip easily on to the bird's leg.

Celluloid rings are ideal for finches and most smaller softbills; aluminium rings are used for budgerigars; stainless steel is preferred for bigger parrots.

Identification of parrots, by means of micro-chipping, is widespread as a means of deterring thieves. The tiny micro-chip with its unique code is implanted into the bird after fledging, and provides a permanent marker. It is activated when a reader is passed over the bird's body.

RINGING A COCKATIEL CHICK

1 It is vital to fit a closed ring before the foot itself is too big for the band to pass over it. Start by grouping the three longest toes together.

2 Next, slide the band over these particular toes, up to the ball of the foot. Note the year of hatching and the individual ring number.

3 Gently slide the ring onwards over the foot, keeping the short back toe parallel with the leg at this stage. Do not rush this procedure.

4 The ring needs to be moved over this toe. Use the blunt end of a matchstick to free the toe. The ring should now move freely over the leg.

As another means of identification, some laboratories carrying out DNA sexing will retain a blood sample of a bird, taken for sexing purposes. This then means that in the future, if the bird is stolen and recovered, it will be possible to prove its identity on the basis of a comparison between the stored DNA sample and a fresh sample. While avian thefts have increased significantly over recent years, this approach offers some hope in the battle against crime of this type.

In the case of budgerigars in particular, you should keep a periodic check on the legs of all your birds

which are fitted with a closed band, to ensure that the leg is not swelling around the ring. This is potentially very serious, if it is not recognized early on, partly because it becomes very difficult to remove the ring. This task should be carried out by an avian vet using specialist tools, and it may be necessary to anaesthetise the bird. There is no known reason as to why budgerigars are especially susceptible, nor indeed as to why this happens. It is more common in the case of birds which have been rung for some time, rather than those which have recently been fitted with rings.

FLEDGING

The period during which young birds leave the nest can be a dangerous time, especially for doves – they leave prematurely, before they are fully able to fly, and have to be watched to ensure they do not become saturated and chilled in heavy rain.

Parrot chicks are normally more developed when they fledge. The risk to them is more from the power of their own flight; Australian parakeets, in particular, are very wild when they fledge, and they can kill themselves by flying hard and fast directly at the aviary mesh. It helps to have screened this area, to show that there is a barrier. The young birds will soon settle down, when transferred to separate accommodation.

Australian parakeets, especially young cock birds, are also at great risk of being attacked by their father, keen to nest again, and so seeking to drive away other males. It is therefore a good idea to remove the first-round chicks as soon as possible, once you are certain that they are capable of feeding on their own.

In other cases however, it may be better to leave the birds together with their parents for a longer period, provided that the aviary is big enough to accommodate the family group.

There are a number of dangers facing a bird which has recently left the nest, even in the confines of an aviary. Young pigeons and doves, in particular, will both fledge before they are able to fly, and if they disappear into undergrowth, they may not be seen by their parents, with the cock bird usually assuming responsibility for attending to their needs at this stage. Young finches, too, are highly vulnerable in wet weather, as their soft plumage can easily become waterlogged, leaving the young birds at risk from hypothermia.

◆ LEFT
Young birds are often duller in terms of their plumage than adults, as in the case of these star finches. It can take anything from a few months to several years for the chicks to attain full coloration.

◆ RIGHT
Young parrot chicks may return to their nest box at night or even during the day, after they have emerged for the first time. Watch for any signs of aggression from the adult pair.

BREEDING PROBLEMS

At each stage in the breeding cycle, problems can arise, some of which will require rapid intervention on your part to save a bird's life.

The first problem that may arise is that the birds may simply show no desire to go to nest. There can be a number of causes, ranging from an incompatible partner to inadequate nesting facilities, so start by reviewing your management of the birds. Try offering other nest sites, in the shelter as well as under cover in the flight. Look at the birds' diet – perhaps a supplement would help to encourage breeding activity. Some birds, even budgerigars, need to be within sight and sound of others of their kind if they are to breed successfully. This can apply to many finches. In the case of bigger parrots, try swapping their partners. The result can be spectacular, with hens going to nest successfully within a few weeks, having failed to make any attempt to nest over previous years.

◆ LEFT
The destructive nature of larger parrots such as cockatoos means that they may destroy their nest box by gnawing at it. Here, the entrance hole has been protected. Check for sharp edges on the metal sheeting, as the birds could cut their tongues or feet badly.

The egg-laying period can create its own problems – notably egg-binding which is a potentially fatal disorder. This occurs when a hen cannot expel the egg from her body and so it forms a blockage, usually in the lower part of the reproductive tract. Chilling, immaturity or old age, and a calcium deficiency are all possible causes of egg-binding. Muscular activity is depressed by the cold, as it is by a deficiency of calcium, while if the egg is abnormally large or has a soft rubbery shell (which can also be a reflection of a lack of calcium), it is more likely to be retained in the body.

The earliest indication of egg-binding is likely to be when the hen

◆ ABOVE AND RIGHT
Feather plucking of chicks in the nest can be a problem, often in the case of the more prolific parrots. Red lories are shown here. The plumage of plucked chicks regrows once they have left the nest.

♦ BELOW
In the case of nervous pairs, or those which
instinctively do not sit tight on their eggs, a
simple heat source in the form of a heat pad
may be required in the nest box.

is seen unexpectedly out of the nest box, and appears to be unsteady on her feet. Her condition will rapidly worsen, and she will lose her ability to perch, ending up huddled on the floor. Emergency veterinary treatment is necessary under these circumstances, with an injection of calcium borogluconate frequently being given to improve muscular contractions, and force the egg out of the reproductive tract.

Should this fail, however, more radical action – possibly surgery – will be required to remove the obstruction. Birds start to recover rapidly from egg-binding, but they should be prevented from laying again until they are fully recovered, which may not be until the next breeding season. In the meantime, try to discover why the problem arose, paying particular attention to the bird's diet.

Although egg-binding is most likely to strike at the start of a clutch, any eggs laid beforehand can be fostered. This also applies if any pairs abandon their nest, but it is important that the eggs are placed under pairs that laid at roughly the same time, to ensure the chicks will be of a similar age when they hatch.

With pheasants and quails, which do not always prove to be good sitters, it may be necessary to invest in an incubator in order to hatch the eggs. Regular turning is essential during the incubation period, and it will help if the incubator incorporates a turning device. Specialist suppliers of such equipment can be found through the columns of bird-keeping magazines, while, in an emergency, a broody bantam may be borrowed to hatch pheasant eggs successfully.

Even in a good breeding season, not all the eggs will hatch. This may be because they were not fertilized at the outset; often the hen retreats immediately into the nest box, and so mating does not take place. These are described as clear eggs because it is possible to see through them when they are held up in front of a bright light. Those eggs that contain well-developed embryos that died late in the incubation period are opaque, and live eggs have a delicate network of blood vessels.

♦ LEFT
Sometimes the nest location may be in an inappropriate site, as here, where it is very close to the covered aviary roof. The heat beneath will be very fierce, especially in warmer climates.

◆ BELOW

Additional seclusion will be needed for nervous pairs when they are nesting. Provide this at the outset of the breeding period, as it can cause birds to desert the nest in their anxiety.

Chilling can be a cause of losses of fertile eggs, while problems with humidity, particularly in incubator surroundings, may have this effect as well. The shell is not actually a solid barrier but consists of many thousands of microscopic pores through which water evaporates during the incubation period. This allows an air-space to form at the blunt end of the egg, and enables the chick to start breathing air about 48 hours prior to hatching. If the rate of evaporation is inadequate, however, the chick will effectively drown in the shell. Another cause of death can be if the shell is heavily contaminated; bacteria pass through the pores and overwhelm the chick's immune system.

Most pairs will feed their chicks without problems, with this task being

undertaken by the hen at first. If the chicks call persistently from within the nest, however, and you discover that something is wrong, you may need to take over, which is not something to be undertaken lightly. It will be a time-consuming occupation. Special hand-rearing foods must be mixed for each feed as instructed on the package. Good hygiene is particularly important. The use of a probiotic preparation, if not incorporated into the rearing food, is advisable to increase the chicks' resistance to infection. A teaspoon with bent sides makes a good feeding nozzle. Wipe the chicks' bills after each feed to prevent any food deposits hardening and distorting the growth of the bill.

Keep the chicks warm in a brooder, gradually reducing the temperature as they grow older and start to feather up. Solid food should be introduced to their diet at this stage, gradually replacing their rearing food. Regular weighing is the best way to monitor progress, bearing in mind that chicks lose weight as they near fledging age.

Feather-plucking of chicks in the nest is a problem confined to budgerigars and lutino cockatiels. There is usually no prior warning. One or both adult birds denude their offspring within a few hours, usually just as the feathers over the back and wings have emerged; in all other respects, they remain exemplary parents. There is nothing that can be done and the plumage will be starting to regrow by the time the chicks leave the nest. Unfortunately, this does appear to be an inherited vice, and such birds are best homed as pets, rather than being kept as part of a breeding programme.

◆ ABOVE

The overwhelming desire of the cock bird to breed may lead to displays of aggression, as shown by this red-winged parakeet. It might be necessary to separate the pair for a short period.

HAND-REARING

1 Spoon feeding is usually a safer and easier method of feeding young parrots. The edges of the spoon are bent inwards to funnel the food down towards the chick's mouth.

2 It is usually possible to see the crop, located at the base of the neck, filling up in this case. Allow the chick to feed at its own pace, and do not rush this process.

3 It is much harder to control the rate of food output if you are using a syringe of any type for hand-feeding. There is also the possibility of a blockage in the nozzle which could create problems.

4 Once they become used to the routine, most young birds will feed without problems. Difficulties are most likely to re-emerge at the start of the weaning period.

Sudden death of young birds can sometimes occur in the post-fledging period, and it is virtually impossible to establish the cause without an autopsy. This can be very valuable, however, to the extent of saving the lives of other birds and alerting you to a health problem in your stock which may otherwise have gone undetected.

In the case of young Australian parakeets and peach-faced lovebirds, which appear unwell soon after they fledge, or are found dead, it is likely that the problem is intestinal worms. The effects of these parasites, acquired while the chicks were picking around in the droppings of the adults, are far more severe at this early stage in life.

Similarly, young budgerigars, which die soon after fledging, are often the victims of the protozoan disease trichomoniasis, having acquired the parasite responsible while being fed by their parents. Treatment of the adult breeding stock will help to prevent further losses, once the cause of the problem has been ascertained.

COLOUR EXPECTATIONS

It is possible to predict the likely outcome of pairings of different colours, based on the laws of genetics. The green budgerigar is dominant over other colours, which means that if a blue is paired with a green, all the offspring will be green but will carry the blue character in their genetic make-up, as shown by the first pairing in the table below. These birds are known as splits (indicated in the tables by the use of an oblique line). When paired together, they should produce a percentage of blue chicks, as shown by the second and third pairings. All such combinations occur randomly, so these are average figures. It is rather like tossing a coin and calling "heads"

or "tails". The results tabled are only a guide but will average out over an increasing number of pairings.

Accurate record-keeping is vital when it comes to colour breeding and managing an exhibition stud. It is

important to have a stock register for such birds, so that you can track their origins and ancestry over a period of time. This will help you to determine which birds should be paired together in the future, and will give you the opportunity to maximise the number of chicks of a particular colour being bred perhaps, or those which are likely to produce youngsters with the best show potential.

The stock register itself will list all the birds which you have in your collection, giving information about their origins, ring numbers, show wins and similar information. It is linked with nest cards on the breeding cages,

♦ BELOW
An opaline olive cock bird, seen on the left, and a young light-green hen. The opaline characteristic is always sex-linked in its mode of inheritance.

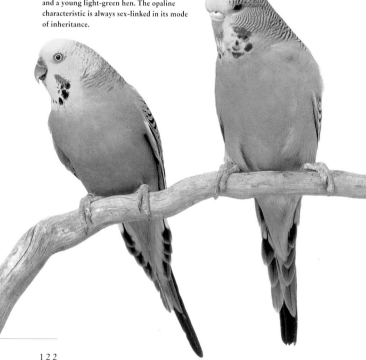

COLOUR EXPECTATIONS

- Green x blue >
  100% green/blue

- Green/blue x green/blue >
  50% green/blue + 25% blue + 25% green

- Green/blue x blue >
  50% green/blue + 50% blue

- Green/blue x green >
  50% green/blue + 50% green

- Blue x blue > 100% blue

SEX-LINKED MUTATIONS

The lutino and cinnamon mutations are sex-linked in their mode of inheritance in budgerigars, as they are in most other birds. The mutation responsible for the change in colour is confined to the sex chromosomes, which determine the individual's gender. This has a direct bearing on the colour expectancy table, because hens have one of their sex chromosomes shorter than the other. This means that, unlike cocks, they cannot be split for a sex-linked mutation. The likely outcomes from the various pairings are therefore:

- Green cock x lutino hen >
  50% green/lutino cocks +
  50% green hens

- Lutino cock x green hen >
  50% green/lutino cocks +
  50% lutino hens

- Green/lutino cock x lutino hen >
  25% green/lutino cocks +

25% lutino cocks + 25% green hens + 25% lutino hens

- Green/lutino cock x green hen >
  25% green cocks +
  25% green/lutino cocks +
  25% green hens + 25% lutino hens

- Lutino cock x lutino hen >
  50% lutino cocks + 50% lutino hens

It is impossible to distinguish split birds by sight from normal greens, but if you want to breed a sex-linked recessive mutation, it is better to choose a cock bird of this type rather than a hen, to give a realistic chance of producing sex-linked chicks. The other advantage of this particular pairing is that it is possible to sex the chicks while they are still in the nest – all the green offspring will be male.

DOMINANT MUTATIONS

The dominant pied mutation, as seen in the budgerigar, is a typical example of dominant mutations. Having one dominant pied bird in a pair means that a percentage of the offspring are likely to be dominant pied. Visual distinction between single and double factor is not usually possible in this case.

- Double factor pied x green =
  100% single factor pied

- Single factor pied x green =
  50% single factor pied +
  50% green

- Single factor pied x double factor pied =
  50% single factor pied +
  50% double factor pied

- Single factor pied x single factor pied =
  50% single factor pied x
  25% double factor pied x
  25% green

- Double factor pied x double factor pied =
  100% double factor

which gives details about the adult pair; the date the first egg was laid; when it is due to hatch; the number of eggs in the clutch; the number of chicks which hatch and any deaths during the rearing period; their colour and ring numbers; and the date when they fledged.

When a pair have finished breeding, these details can be transferred to a breeding register, which enables you to monitor the breeding progress of particular birds – exhibition hopefuls, for example – and the chicks which are retained in the stud are listed in due course in the stock register. You can purchase registers in printed form, or as computer programmes. Printed nest cards are also available, although alternatively, you can simply write or print these yourself.

◆ RIGHT
A young cobalt dominant pied cock seen with a young light-green hen. Although the barring on the forehead of both birds will recede at the first moult, the pied markings on the cock will remain constant.

GLOSSARY

Albino a bird that has no colour pigment and so is pure white with pink eyes

Aviary outdoor housing for birds, consisting of a flight area with a built-in shelter

Aviculture the study and breeding of birds that are not regarded as domesticated

Bird a warm-blooded creature characterized by the presence of feathers on its body; reproduces by means of hard-shelled eggs

Birdroom indoor housing for birds, often used for breeding purposes or for winter housing of delicate species

Breed domestic variant, usually a colour variant created by selective breeding

Buff a term used mainly in the canary fancy for birds that have coarse feathers (as distinct from Yellow)

Cap the area at the top of the bird's head, which may be coloured differently from the surrounding area

Cere the area above the bill, which includes the nostrils; especially significant for sexing budgerigars

Clear a pure-coloured light canary, such as a yellow or white; also used for an egg which fails to hatch because it was not fertilized

Cloaca the terminal portion of the digestive tract, where the urinary and reproductive tracts also open, with their contents passing out through the vent

Closed ring a ring that is slid over a chick's foot while it is still in the nest, as a means of confirming its age

Colony system housing and breeding birds of the same species in groups

Colour feeding the use of particular foods when certain birds, such as some finches and canaries, are moulting;

colour foods maintain the colour of the new plumage, and are available as a softfood or as a liquid

Conure a member of a group of parakeets occurring in parts of Central and South America

Crestbred a chick bred from crested stock that is not crested itself

Crop the part of the avian digestive tract at the base of the neck, where food is stored before being passed down through the digestive system

Dead-in-the-shell a chick that develops up to the point of hatching but fails to break out of the egg

Double buffing pairing of two birds with a buff feather type, which may create the impression of a larger bird; carries the risk of feather cysts

Down light, fluffy feathering which lies close to the body, providing insulation; most readily seen in chicks

Egg-binding condition arising from the failure of a hen to lay an egg, so that it remains trapped in her body

Eggfood food given to adult birds, especially canaries, to help them rear their chicks

Enteritis inflammation of the digestive tract; may be a number

of causes, but typically results in greenish droppings and can be life-threatening

Fancy selective breeding to display traits for exhibition purposes

Feather cysts swellings, typically over the back of canaries caused by repeated double-buffing, with the feathers being too soft and large to emerge from the feather shaft under the skin

Finch seed-eating bird

Flecking undesirable dark flecks on the feathers, typically seen on the head of budgerigars

Fledging the stage at which a young bird leaves the nest

Fledgling the name given to a young bird that has just left the nest

Foul clear areas on an otherwise self bird, notably a canary

Flight panel the section of an aviary that, when assembled, will create the flight area

Fostering transferring eggs or chicks from one pair of birds to another

French moult viral illness especially affecting young budgerigars, causing them to loose their flight and tail feathers; treatment is available

Frugivore a bird that feeds mainly on fresh fruit

Gizzard the part of the digestive tract where foodstuffs such as seed are broken down

Going light weight loss causing the breastbone at the front of the body to become more prominent; often indicative of long-standing illness in the bird

Grit small fragments of oystershell and tiny stones provided to assist the digestion of food in the gizzard; may sometimes be mixed with other ingredients such as powdered charcoal

Gut-loading providing food of high nutritional value to invertebrates which in turn will be fed to birds

Hand-rearing/raising the rearing of young birds by hand

Hybridization the breeding together of two closely related birds

In-breeding mating of two closely related individuals; often son and mother or daughter and father

Insectivore a bird that feeds on invertebrates as part of its diet

Invertebrate creature without a backbone

Iris the coloured circular area surrounding the black pupil in the centre of the eye

Iron storage disease illness resulting from absorption of excessive amounts of iron, especially common in softbills such as toucans and touracos

Livefood invertebrates used as bird food

Moult the shedding of new feathers, which are replaced by new ones

Mule the name given to hybrid chicks bred from canary x Eurasian finch pairings

Nectivore a bird that feeds mainly on nectar as part of its diet

Normal the natural colour form, such as grey in the case of the cockatiel

Outcrossing pairing to avoid breeding between a related cock and hen bird

Parrot a member of the order Psittaciformes

Plainhead a canary of a crested variety bred without a crest; used for pairings with crested individuals

Probiotic a product containing beneficial bacteria; of particular value in the case of young birds being hand-reared, or those recovering from illness

Protozoa microscopic single-celled creatures, which can be implicated in cases of digestive disturbances

Psittacine a description meaning parrot-like, often used as a collective term for members of this group

Scurvy a condition resulting from a dietary deficiency of Vitamin C; it is a rare condition, but may be seen in certain birds, such as toucans

Self a solid-coloured, dark canary such as a green or blue individual

Sex-linked a genetic characteristic associated with the pair of sex chromosomes

Sexual dimorphism a term used to describe birds in which it is possible to distinguish the sexes by differences in their appearance

Show standard the ideal example of a particular domesticated bird, which serves as a guide for judging at shows;

specifies not just the physical appearance but also other features, such as coloration, for which points are awarded

Show stud a group of birds, the majority of which are related, being kept for exhibition purposes

Soaked seed seed that has been soaked in water and then washed off before being fed to the birds; often used as a rearing food, with millet sprays being valued for this purpose

Softbill a bird that does not feed predominantly on bird seed

Softfood bird food that is not comprised of seed; includes softbill food and eggfood

Split ring a ring that can be applied to the leg at any stage in a bird's life; used for identification purposes rather than as a guarantee of age

Surgical sexing sexing of a bird by viewing its body organs through an instrument, usually an endoscope

Ticked a canary term used to describe a bird that has just a small amount of dark feathering on an otherwise clear background

Tight feather sleek plumage

Type the appearance of the bird, as specified for judging purposes

Unflighted a young bird, usually a canary, that has yet to moult its flight feathers

Variegated a bird that has relatively even dark and light areas of plumage

Vent the orifice through which the cloaca connects to the outside world

Yellow the colour of a bird (typically a budgerigar or canary) that has a more colourful plumage than a buff individual

Yolk sac part of the egg that provides the chick with nutrition prior to and immediately after hatching

ACKNOWLEDGEMENTS

The author and publishers would like to thank the following for their help and co-operation in making this book:
Ghalib Al-Nasser; Dennis Avon; Paul and June Bailey; Fred Barnicoat; Henk Branje; E. F. Cannon; Harry Carr; Irene Christie; Stuart Christophers; Dave Coles; John Daniels; Alain and Janine Delille; Philip Dobinson; Alan Donnelly; Joseph Forshaw; Ken Griggs; Steve Hailey; Barry Hammond; John and Sharon Harris; Harold and Mary Haslam; William Horsfield; Jos Hubers; Graeme Hyde; Colin Jackson; Alan Jones; Ernst Kruger; Peter and Connie Landry; Kees Lansen; Cyril Laubscher; Errol Laubscher; E. R. Lemon; George and Jill Lewsey; Leon Malan; Chris Mason; Stanley Maughan; Jan Muller; Doug Nudd; Arthur O'Bray; Ron Oxley; Roderick Parrish; Nathan Reynolds; Danny Roels; Max Sanderson; Francesca Sherfield; Stan Sindel; Harry Stephan; Rebecca Taylor; Tony Tilford; George Urquhart; Peggy Winser; Michael Woods.

PICTURE CREDITS

t=top; b=bottom; c=centre; l=left; r=right

Dennis Avon 1; 2; 3; 34cr; 35br; 39cl; 39c; 39bl; 39bc; 39br; 41t; 41cl; 41c; 41cr; 41bl; 41bc; 41br; 43cl; 43c; 43cr; 43bl; 43bc; 43br; 44br; 49; 70t; 72cl; 72bc; 72br; 84bl; 84bc; 84br; 93bl; 93br; 105tl; 105tc; 105tr; 107tr; 109tc; 109tr; 114tl; 114tr; 114bl; 114br.

Cyril Laubscher 5; 4; 7b; 8–9; 10; 11; 12; 13tr; 13b; 14t; 14b; 15t; 15b; 16; 17; 22; 23t; 23bc; 23br; 25t; 25b; 26; 27; 30t; 30b; 31t; 31b; 32t; 32b; 33b; 35bl; 36; 40t; 40b; 42; 44t; 45t; 46c; 47t; 47bl; 48t; 50t; 50bl; 51t; 51br; 52; 53; 59; 60; 62c; 62bl; 62bc; 63t; 63b; 64c; 68; 69; 70b; 71tl; 71tr; 71b; 73tl; 73tr; 73br; 74t; 74b; 75t; 75bl; 76t; 76b; 77t; 77b; 78; 80t; 80c; 80bl; 80br; 81bc; 81br; 82t; 82cl; 82cr; 82bl; 82br; 83tc; 83tr; 83bl; 83br; 84t; 85tc; 85tr; 85bl; 85br; 86; 87tl; 87tc; 87b; 88; 89t; 89b; 90; 91; 92b; 93tl; 93tc; 93cl; 93cr; 93tr;

94t; 94bl; 94br; 95tl; 95tr; 95b; 96t; 96b; 97t; 97b; 98; 99; 100t; 100b; 101t; 101b; 102; 103; 104b; 105c; 105b; 106t; 106c; 106bl; 106br; 107tl; 107b; 108t; 108c; 108b; 109c; 109br; 110t; 110b; 111t; 111b; 112t; 112bl; 112br; 113t; 113c; 113bl; 113br; 115t; 115bl; 115bc; 115br; 116tc; 116tr; 116bc; 116br; 117t; 117bl; 117br; 118t; 118b; 119t; 119b; 120t; 120b; 121b; 121tl; 121tr; 121bl; 121br, 124, 125, 126, 127, 128.

SUPPLIERS

UNITED KINGDOM
Birkett Fencing
Frizington
Cumbria CA26 3XS
Tel: (01946) 861420

Ernest Charles
Copplestone
Crediton
Devon EX17 2YZ
Tel: (01363) 84842

Grange Aviaries & Pet Centre
Woodhouse Lane
Botley
Southampton SO30 2EZ
Tel: (01489) 781260

Oaklands Park Farm Aviaries
Patridge Lane
Nr Newdigate
Surrey RH5 5BU
Tel: (01293) 871408

Livefoods Direct
Houghton Road
North Anston Trading Estate
Sheffield S25 4JJ
Tel: (01909) 518888

Safari Select
Warren Farm
Sundridge
Kent TN14 6EE
Tel: (01959) 562193

Southern Aviaries
Tinkers Lane
Hadlow Down
Uckfield
East Sussex TN22 4EU
Tel: (01825) 830283

UNITED STATES
Contact the following web pages for the latest information regarding mail order supplies of bird cages, bird foods, bird toys, breeder suppliers, bird treats and products:
www.birdsnways.com
www.creativebird.com
www.hornbecks.com
www.pets.com
www.wildwingsorganic.com

AUSTRALIA
Australian Bird Co. & Breeding Farm
578 Springvale Road
Springvale South
VIC 3172
Tel: (03) 9548 2422

Bird Man
1964 Wanneroo Road
Weerabup
WA 6031
Tel: (06) 9407 5090

Pet City
224 Wishart Road
Mt Gravatt
QLD 4122
Tel: (04) 3349 2086

East Dunbartonshire Council

Pets Paradise
Shop 35, Gilchrist Drive
Campbelltown
NSW 2560
Tel: (02) 46325 2855

Oxford Pet Supplies
350 Oxford Street
Bondi Junction
NSW 2022
Tel: (02) 9389 9294

FURTHER READING

*Although some of the books listed below may
be out of print, they can often be obtained
from public libraries, or from secondhand
bookstores specializing in aviculture titles.*

Alderton, D. (1988) *A Birdkeeper's Guide
to Budgies*, Tetra Press

Alderton, D. (1988) *A Birdkeeper's Guide
to Finches*, Tetra Press

Alderton, D. (1989) *A Birdkeeper's Guide
to Parakeets*, Tetra Press

Alderton, D. (1989) *A Birdkeeper's Guide
to Parrots & Macaws*, Tetra Press

Alderton, D. (1989) *A Birdkeeper's Guide
to Cockatiels*, Tetra Press

Alderton, D. (1990) *A Birdkeeper's Guide
to Breeding Birds*, Tetra Press

Alderton, D. (1990) *A Birdkeeper's Guide
to Cockatoos*, Tetra Press

Alderton, D. (1991) *The Atlas of Parrots*,
T. F. H. Publications

Alderton, D. (1992) *You & Your Pet Bird*,
Dorling Kindersley

Alderton, D. (1995) *The Handbook of
Cage and Aviary Birds*, Blandford Press

Alderton, D. (1998) *The Complete Guide
to Bird Care*, Howell Book House

Alderton, D. (2000) *The Complete Book
of Finches and Softbills: Their Care and
Breeding*, T. F. H. Publications

Bielfeld, H. (1988) *Canaries and Related
Birds*, T. F. H. Publications

Bracegirdle, J. (1981) *The Border Fancy
Canary*, Saiga Publishing

Cole, B. H. (1985) *Avian Medicine and
Surgery*, Blackwell Scientific Publications

Cooke, D. & F. (1987) *Keeping Cockatiels
– A Complete Guide*, Blandford Press

Cross, J. S. (1978) *The Gloster Fancy
Canary*, Saiga Publishing

Dodwell, G. T. (1982) *The Lizard Canary
and Other Rare Breeds*, Triplegate

Goodwin, D. (1982) *Estrildid Finches of
the World*, British Museum
(Natural History)

Harper, D. (1986) *Pet Birds for Home and
Garden*, Salamander Books

Hayward, J. (1979) *Lovebirds and Their
Colour Mutations*, Blandford Press

Howman, K. C. R. (1979) *Pheasants –
Their Breeding and Management*,
K & R Books

Howson, E. (1980) *The Yorkshire Canary*,
Saiga Publishing

Immelmann, K. (1982) *Australian Finches*,
Angus and Robertson

Low, R. (1977) *Lories and Lorikeets*,
Paul Elek

Low, R. (1986) *Parrots – Their Care and
Breeding*, Blandford Press

Low, R. (1992) *Parrots in Aviculture –
A Photo Reference Guide*, Blandford Press

Mobbs, A. (1985) *Gouldian Finches*,
Nimrod

Restall, R. L. (1975) *Finches and Other
Seed-eating Birds*, Faber and Faber

Robbins, G. E. S. (1984) *Quail – Their
Breeding and Management*,
World Pheasant Association

Smith, G. A. (1979) *Encyclopedia
of Cockatiels*, T. F. H. Publications

Trollope, J. (1983) *The Care and Breeding
of Seed-eating Birds*, Blandford Press

Vince, C. (1980) *Keeping Softbilled Birds*,
Stanley Paul

Walker, G. B. R. & Avon, Dennis (1987)
Coloured, Type & Song Canaries,
Blandford Press

INDEX

aging birds 72–3
aviaries
  assembling 28–9
  cleaning 65, 79
  furnishing 30–1
  making 24–5
  ready-made 22–3
  siting 14–15, 26–7
  specialized 34–5

bathing 57, 59, 88
birdrooms 32–3
breeding 100–1, 110–11, 122–3
  problems 118–21
budgerigars (*Melopsittacus erithacus*) 8, 18, 23, 34, 38, 72, 89
  breeding 100, 110, 111, 114, 118, 120
  feeding 37, 43, 62, 64
  pets 8, 55, 56, 57, 58
  showing 91, 92–3
bumblefoot 20

cages 13, 17, 18–19, 21, 54, 56–7
canaries 8, 18, 23, 39, 40, 56, 92
  breeding 99, 104, 105, 108, 110, 111
catching birds 66–7
cereals 40–1
chicks 113–14, 115
claw trimming 84
cockatiels (*Nymphicus hollandicus*) 23, 45, 100
cockatoos 9, 23, 83
collecting birds 70–1, 72–3, 74–5, 76–7
colour 50–1, 122–3
cordon bleus 76
cuttlefish bone 43, 110

disease 20, 27, 34, 48, 59, 65, 73, 75, 81, 82, 79, 83, 86–7, 88, 89, 108
  egg-binding 110, 118–19
door fastenings 21
doves 8, 61, 76

breeding 104, 106, 107, 108, 111, 119
  diamond (*Geopelia cuneata*) 72, 76
drinking 57

eggs 110–11, 118–20
eye problems 82

feather plucking 11, 19, 59, 83, 88, 120–1
feeding 53
  aviary birds 62–3, 74
  chicks 113–14, 115, 120, 121
  nectar-eaters 46, 63, 74
  seed-eaters 38–45
finches 8, 11, 13, 14, 16, 23, 33, 88, 91, 92, 100
  breeding 102, 104, 105, 113, 116, 118
  bullfinch (*Pyrrhula pyrrhula*) 39
  cut-throat (*Amadina fasciata*) 103
  feeding 38, 62, 64
  zebra (*Poephila guttata*) 73, 91, 100, 120
fledging 117
flight cages 17, 18–19, 21
flights 17, 61
French moult 83
fruit 44–5

greenstuff 44–5
grit 43
gut loading 48

handling birds 66–7
hatching 113
health, assessing 62, 72–3, 80
hen birds, egg-bound 110, 118–19
humming-birds 9, 46, 49, 63

incubation 110–11, 112
injuries 84–5
insects, as food 48–9

larvae, as food 48–9
lice 86, 87, 88
livefood 48–9
lorikeets and lories 46
lost birds 67

macaws 13, 15, 23
mesh 23
micro-chip implantation 116
mites 73, 79, 86, 88, 108
moulting 50–1
mynahs 19, 20, 45, 47, 57, 99

nectar-feeders 37, 46, 63, 74
nesting facilities 104–9

obesity 18, 20
oil seeds 38–9

parakeets 8, 28, 25, 60, 75, 76, 77, 89, 117
  Indian ring-necked 14, 84
parasites, external 79, 86–7
parasites, internal 27, 34, 48, 75, 87
parrots 8, 11, 12, 15, 18, 20, 21, 25, 33, 46, 67, 70, 100, 102
  breeding 99, 106, 110, 116, 118
  eclectus (*Eclectus roratus*) 63
  feeding 37, 38, 39, 40, 44, 45, 48, 62–3
  grey 20, 70, 72
  health 83, 88
  pets 54, 55, 56, 57, 58–9
  Senegal (*Poicephalus senegalus*) 23
PBFD (psittacine beak and feather disease) 83
perches 20
pheasants 8, 35, 41, 44, 63, 65, 67, 76
  breeding 108, 111, 114, 119
pigeons 61, 76
  breeding 104, 107, 108, 113
plants, poisonous 55
playstands 13, 55
pseudotuberculosis 65

quails 35, 41, 62, 63, 65, 76
  breeding 104, 107, 108, 111, 119

ringing 116, 121
rodents 14, 23, 26, 32, 62, 65
roundworms 73, 75, 87

safety, pet birds 55
scaly face 73
seeds 38–9, 40–1, 42
sexing birds 102-3
showing 92–3, 94–5, 96–7
sick birds, care 81
snakes 15, 26
softbills 12, 14, 16, 35, 61, 74, 88, 91
  breeding 99, 104, 116
  feeding 37, 38, 44, 47, 48, 49, 62–3
starlings 57, 99
sunbirds 46, 99

talking 11, 59
taming 58–9
tanagers 47, 98
tapeworms 75, 87
termites 15
touraco 35, 44, 47
tumours 73, 89

viruses 83

water 57, 64–5
waxbills 48, 76, 113
wild birds 14, 23
worms, as food 48–9

NOTES

NOTES

NOTES

NOTES